GREAT LIVES FROM GOD'S

A Man of Integrity and Forgiveness

JOSEPH

Profiles in Character from

CHARLES R. SWINDOLL

THOMAS NELSON
Since 1798

NASHVILLE   DALLAS   MEXICO CITY   RIO DE JANEIRO

Published in Nashville, Tennessee, by Thomas Nelson. Thomas Nelson is a registered trademark of Thomas Nelson, Inc.

Thomas Nelson, Inc. titles may be purchased in bulk for educational, business, fund-raising, or sales promotional use. For information, please e-mail SpecialMarkets@ThomasNelson.com.

All Scripture quotations in this book, except those noted otherwise, are from the New American Standard Bible © 1960, 1962, 1963, 1971, 1973, 1975, and 1977 by the Lockman Foundation, and are used by permission.

Other Scripture quotations are from the following sources:

The New International Version of the Bible (NIV), © 1983 by the International Bible Society. Used by permission of Zondervan Bible Publishers.

The Living Bible (LB), © 1971 by Tyndale House Publishers, Wheaton, Ill. Used by permission.

The King James Version of the Bible (KJV).

ISBN 978-0-8499-1342-6 (HC)
ISBN 978-1-4002-8014-8 (SE)
ISBN 978-1-4002-8033-9 (trade paper)

Printed and bound in the United States of America

HB 02.20.2024

JOSEPH

A Man of Integrity and Forgiveness

Publications by Charles R. Swindoll

ADULT BOOKS

Active Spirituality

The Bride

Compassion: Showing We Care
  in a Careless World

The Darkness and the Dawn

David: A Man of Passion
  and Destiny

Day by Day

Dear Graduate

Dropping Your Guard

Elijah: A Man of Heroism
  and Humility

Encourage Me

Esther: A Woman of Strength
  and Dignity

The Finishing Touch

Flying Closer to the Flame

For Those Who Hurt

God's Provision

The Grace Awakening

Growing Deep in the Christian Life

Growing Strong in the Seasons of Life

Growing Wise in Family Life

Hand Me Another Brick

Home: Where Life Makes Up Its Mind

Hope Again

Improving Your Serve

Intimacy with the Almighty

Killing Giants, Pulling Thorns

Laugh Again

Leadership: Influence That Inspires

Living Above the Level of Mediocrity

Living Beyond the Daily Grind,
  Books I and II

The Living Insights Study Bible—
  General Editor

Living on the Ragged Edge

Make Up Your Mind

Man to Man

Moses: A Man of Selfless Dedication

The Mystery of God's Will

The Quest for Character

Recovery: When Healing Takes Time

The Road to Armageddon

Sanctity of Life

Simple Faith

Simple Trust

Starting Over

Start Where You Are

Strengthening Your Grip

Stress Fractures

Strike the Original Match

The Strong Family

Suddenly One Morning

The Tale of the Tardy Oxcart

Three Steps Forward, Two Steps Back

Victory: A Winning Game Plan for Life

Why, God?

You and Your Child

DEDICATION

It is with overwhelming feelings of gratitude
that I dedicate this book to
JACK A. TURPIN
who has served on the Board of Incorporate Members
of
Dallas Theological Seminary
faithfully, diligently, unselfishly
since 1981.

All of us in the Seminary family
give God great praise
for his
model of integrity,
spirit of generosity,
heart of humility,
and commitment to his family.

CONTENTS

CONTENTS

INTRODUCTION

The tragedy of our times drove me to read a fascinating book. Finding myself weary of all the tabloids exploiting scandalous rumors and investigative reports that dig into the cellars of people's private lives, I needed fresh hope that genuine heroes still exist, that some remain who model greatness, that some are still worth our respect and admiration.

So I put everything else on hold as I sat down and read David Aikman's fine volume, *Great Souls*. In less than 400 pages, based on personal observation and meticulous research, Aikman reminds his readers that indeed there are at least six great individuals who have helped change the twentieth century by their personal lives and remarkable achievements. In spite of their own imperfections and weaknesses, these very human individuals rose above their circumstances, overcame enormous obstacles, and committed themselves to wholesome goals with overpowering determination.

As I finished the book I realized anew the value of human biography. Who isn't inspired by a man or woman who exerts phenomenal and beneficial influence? Who can read about someone's courage to stand alone with single-minded vision amidst a slippery ever-eroding culture, and not want to emulate such a life? I also found myself stimulated with fresh desire to continue this published series of biblical biographies I began over a year ago—first David's, then Esther's.

No collection titled "Great Lives from God's Word" would be complete without its including Joseph, a man who modeled a life anyone would consider great. As I write that statement, it seems necessary that we understand what I mean by "great." Having just finished his book with a title that includes the word itself, the comments of David Aikman return to mind:

> The word *great* has many different definitions, but among them are "prominent, renowned . . . eminent, distinguished . . . lofty, noble, magnanimous . . . assiduous, persistent . . . wonderful, admirable" [*Webster's Third New International Dictionary*]. The list goes on. In a thesaurus, under *magnanimous*, one also finds "great of heart or soul" [*Roget's International Thesaurus*].[1]

And then, he elaborates with these very personal reflections, with which I heartily agree:

> I have always personally been inspired by the lives of great people. It is hard not to be energized by the stories of how individuals have risen above adversity or suffering, or have maintained a purity in the face of great temptation. Our age, with its habit of instantly judging a man or woman's life based on the fragmentary and proverbial sound bite, is often impatient with detail, nuances, depth.[2]

Not wanting to demonstrate such impatience, I've taken the time to push the "pause button" alongside each life in this series in order to examine carefully and appreciate fully what could be missed by the hurried reader. I intend to maintain the same standard in this examination of Joseph. After all, when we discover that his story occupies more space in the book of Genesis than any other single individual—more than Adam, Noah, Abraham, Isaac, or even his own father, Jacob—we realize we're not dealing with some obscure lesser light. On the contrary, here is one of the ancient patriarchs whose presence casts a sizeable shadow across the colorful landscape of Hebrew history. Here is one on the list of God's "greats" . . . a life lived for His glory and, equally significant, though he was terribly mistreated, lived high above the all-too-common reactions of rage, resentment, and revenge. Here is one who deliberately chose to overlook unfair offenses, to overcome enormous obstacles, and model a virtue that is fast becoming lost in our hostile age—*forgiveness*. But more on that later.

I am again indebted to several faithful and gifted folks for assisting me in getting this volume into your hands. David Moberg has demonstrated a balanced blend of thoughtful understanding and gentle persuasion in helping me stay at the task. Helen Peters has once again deciphered my handwritten tablet sheets and turned these lines into correctly spelled and accurately punctuated words, sentences, and paragraphs, as well as secured all the required permissions for the footnotes. Judith Markham, my keen-eyed editor, has applied her very capable skills to yet another of my volumes, working diligently against the demands and deadlines we faced in this project. In addition to those "great souls," I want to thank two of my colleagues at our Insight for Living offices in Anaheim, Gary Matlack and Wendy Peterson, for their willingness to look over my shoulder and, when necessary, save me from historical error, verbal misstatement, or technical mistake. Lee Hough's excellent work on our study guide to this book was extremely helpful on several occasions, and I gratefully acknowledge my appreciation for his careful research and creative skills.

I owe a special debt of gratitude to Cynthia, my wife of more than 43 years, whose encouragement keeps my pen moving and whose support and understanding know no bounds. Because of her especially, and all those mentioned above, *Joseph: A Man of Integrity and Forgiveness* is now available, and I, a man of tired hand and weary mind, am relieved.

CHUCK SWINDOLL
Dallas, Texas

A Man of Integrity and Forgiveness

JOSEPH

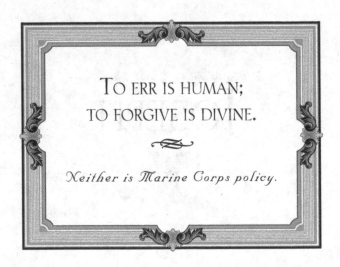

To err is human;
to forgive is divine.

Neither is Marine Corps policy.

CHAPTER ONE

Favored Son, Hated Brother

I couldn't help but smile when the slogan on the page to the left fell into my hands out of an envelope that also contained the letter from a former military friend. He and I both knew, from experience, that those eight bold words did indeed represent an unwritten policy of the marines—at least the "old corps" of which we were once a part. I understand it's changing these days (frankly, I'll believe it when I see it). If so, such changes are long overdue.

Changes regarding forgiveness may be occurring in the ranks of the marines, but they aren't among the ranks of humanity. "I don't get mad, I get even" isn't merely a harmless bumper sticker that makes people smile; it's a strong statement of painful reality. How else can we explain the proliferation of lawsuits, the short fuses of American drivers, or the explosive reactions and sometimes deadly retaliations of those who feel they've been wronged? "Getting even" has reached the level of a twisted art form in our hostile society. Humans do err, and God does forgive. But neither represents a policy most folks are willing to accept.

Thankfully, there are exceptions. Every once in a while we happen upon a life that boldly represents a contrast to the lowest common denominator of today's low-level majority opinion. Occasionally, such a person emerges, and we are stunned by his or her greatness.

This happened to me back in 1980. I decided early in the summer to read the Bible through from Genesis to Revelation before the end of that year. I hadn't finished even the first book of the Scriptures before I met a biblical character whose life caused me to shake my head in amazement time after time. Regardless of how he was treated, in spite of unfair and erroneous accusations, even though he was rejected, abandoned, abused, maligned, and forgotten, he refused to become resentful or bear a grudge or succumb to bitterness. To be completely truthful with you, he seemed too good to be real. So I read his story again—this time much more slowly and deliberately. To my amazement, a more careful reading revealed an even deeper level of patience and purity. I vowed then that someday I would return to that life recorded in Genesis 37 through 50, and, with pen in hand, introduce him to the general public. Here was a man all should meet!

That time has come. At long last, it is my privilege to introduce you to a man of enormous integrity who modeled continual forgiveness. His name is Joseph. Unless I miss my guess, you will never forget this man. But why should we be surprised? His biography is found in the single most astounding book ever written—the Bible. No life recorded there is either unimportant or forgettable.

> The Bible is the supreme Book on human personality. . . . From Adam in Genesis to Satan in the Apocalypse, its portraits are unforgettable. . . . Augustine wrote how men wander over the earth and wonder at the rivers and the mountains and the sea and the stars, while all the time man himself is the great wonder. . . . How fearful and how wonderful are man's terrible and glorious capacities and possibilities. . . . It is said that every man's life contains sufficient material for a great novel.[1]

GOD'S TRAINING MANUAL

God constantly uses the lives of Bible characters to teach us, to encourage us, to warn us. Who can forget the impact of the truths lived out in the lives of David and Esther, of Moses and Jonah, of Peter and Paul? It's impossible to leave truth in the theoretical realm when you see it revealed in the lives of real-life men and women. That is what these divinely inspired biographies do; they distill truth and weave it into the fabric of everyday living. God's training manual is full of lives that inspire and instruct.

Romans 15:4 states, "For whatever was written *in earlier times* was written for our instruction, that through perseverance and the encouragement of the Scriptures we might have hope" (emphasis added). This reference to "earlier times" encompasses all the truths written in the Old Testament. And if I read this verse correctly, there are two basic reasons God has allowed us to have the Old Testament available for study and application: first, for present instruction, and second, for future hope. God has given us this information so that our minds can learn the truth about Him and about life, and so that we will be encouraged to persevere in the future.

Then, 1 Corinthians 10, verses 6 and 11 say: "Now *these things* happened as examples for us, that we should not crave evil things, as they also craved. . . . Now *these things* happened to them as an example, and they were written for our instruction, upon whom the ends of the ages have come" (emphasis added). "These things" in verse 6 refer to the first five verses of that chapter, which point back to the people of Israel and some of the things they endured and experienced. The same thought is then repeated in verse 11, emphasizing that God has given us Old Testament truths to instruct us, to give us hope, and to warn us about how we are to live day by day, so that we might not crave the evil things some of our spiritual ancestors craved.

Earlier I quoted Clarence Edward Macartney's statement that concludes with the comment that everyone's life has the makings of a novel. Perhaps no life in the Bible reads more like a suspenseful and compelling novel than Joseph's.

> Joseph's story is a finely wrought and self-contained novella, describing in vivid detail the development of his character from charismatic and arrogant youth to compassionate middle age. . . . Genesis reaches a melo-dramatic peak in these climactic last chapters: a riches-to-rags-to-riches

tale replete with every human passion—love and hate, ambition and glory, jealousy and fury. Tears of joy and grief are shed. Garments are rent in anguish. It's a gripping saga of treachery and deception, betrayal and forgiveness.[2]

A BRIEF OVERVIEW

Before we get better acquainted with Joseph, let's take a quick glance at some background information. It will help if you remember that his biography falls neatly into three distinct segments.

- *Birth to Seventeen Years* (Genesis 30:24–37:2)
  During this time Joseph's family was in transition—everyone was unsettled, on the move. A low-level antagonism was brewing as his family clashed and argued in jealousy and hatred.

- *Seventeen to Thirty Years* (Genesis 37:2–41:46)
  This second segment occurs as Joseph reaches young manhood. It seems as though his life becomes out of control. Enslavement, unfair accusation, and imprisonment assault him.

- *Thirty Years to Death* (Genesis 41:46–50:26)
  Joseph's last eighty years are years of prosperity and reward under God's blessing. He had the classic opportunity to get even with his brothers, to ruin them forever, but he refused. Instead he blessed, protected, and forgave.

Jacob: the Aging Father

The first person we encounter (and need to understand) is Joseph's father, Jacob. His other name is Israel which means "God strives"—a name given to him after he wrestled with God and clung to Him for a blessing. (The story is recorded in Genesis 32:22–32.) This name is a significant improvement over his original name, Jacob, which literally meant "chiseler" or "deceiver." We will come back to that in a moment, but for now, read the opening lines of Genesis 37 slowly and carefully:

Now Jacob lived in the land where his father had sojourned, in the land of Canaan. These are the records of the generations of Jacob. Joseph, when seventeen years of age, was pasturing the flock with his brothers while he was still a youth, along with the sons of Bilhah and the sons of Zilpah, his father's wives. And Joseph brought back a bad report about them to their father. Now Israel loved Joseph more than all his sons, because he was the son of his old age; and he made him a varicolored tunic.

Genesis 37:1–3

Jacob was an aging man when Joseph was born. The Scriptures declare that Joseph was "the son of his old age." Jacob's original name, "deceiver," was appropriate since that had been his nature from the time he was a very young man. It is not surprising, then, that deception was part of the on-going problem in his family later in his life.

Not only was Jacob a deceiver, we shall also see that he was a passive father. Here, in this ancient story, is a classic illustration of a man who was too busy for his family, too preoccupied and unconcerned, which meant he was too passive to deal with what was occurring in the lives of any of his children.

Because Jacob was getting up in years at this time, he loved Joseph to the utmost. When Joseph was born, Jacob got a new lease on life. We often witness that today when men in their late forties or older become fathers. When that happens, older fathers seem to gain a new incentive to rearrange their lives. And that's what happened to Jacob when Joseph was born. Furthermore, his great love for Joseph was underscored by the fact that he was the child of Jacob's beloved wife, Rachel.

A few chapters earlier we read these words about Joseph's birth.

Then God remembered Rachel, and God gave heed to her and opened her womb. So she conceived and bore a son and said, "God has taken away my reproach." And she named him Joseph, saying, "May the LORD give me another son."

Genesis 30:22–24

His mother gave him the name Joseph, which means "add to me," or "may He [God] add." Rachel was saying, "May the LORD give me another son."

Until Joseph was born, Rachel had been barren, and the greatest stigma for a woman of her culture was sterility. For a woman to be married and to live out her life without children was a disgrace to her and often to her husband. In this case, however, it was not a stigma for Jacob, because he already had children by his first wife, Leah, who also happened to be Rachel's sister. That brings up another interesting story. Stay with me through a few details. It will help you appreciate and understand what Joseph experienced early in life.

When Jacob was a young man, he fell in love with Rachel, the beautiful daughter of a man named Laban. "If I can marry your daughter Rachel," Jacob promised Laban, "I will work for you faithfully for seven years." The bargain was struck, and Jacob served out his seven years. But on Jacob's wedding day, Laban pulled a switch; he tricked Jacob. He deceived the deceiver, some might say, and Jacob ended up married to Leah, Rachel's older and less attractive sister.

When Jacob realized what had happened, he said, "I will work seven more years for Rachel." Understand, she was the woman he really loved. So Laban gave him Rachel as his second wife, and Jacob worked another seven years for his father-in-law. Obviously, this family was not off to a good start!

Within the next few years, Leah bore Jacob seven children—six sons and one daughter. As a result of Leah and Rachel's competition for his affection and for motherhood, he also bore four sons by his wives' handmaidens.

During all this, Rachel pleaded with God to open her womb, to give her a child. Finally God remembered her and gave them Joseph.

By now, Jacob had worked twenty long years for his father-in-law and was eager to be on his way. Laban lived in Haran, a land far to the northeast of Canaan, and Jacob wanted to take his wives and his family back to his homeland, the land of Canaan, commonly referred to as the Promised Land.

Now it came about when Rachel had borne Joseph, that Jacob said to Laban, "Send me away, that I may go to my own place and to my own country. Give me my wives and my children for whom I have served you, and let me depart; for you yourself know my service which I have rendered you."

Genesis 30:25–26

Canaan: The Promised Land

"Canaan is where I belong," Jacob said to his father-in-law. "That's where my people have their roots. That's where I want to rear my children."

Laban agreed, but in the process, once again, he and Jacob both tried to deceive each other. Finally, however, Jacob and his family made their way back to the land of Canaan—but not without tragedy. The first incident occurred when they got to the city of Shechem, in an area populated by the people known as the Hivites. Read and weep:

Now Dinah the daughter of Leah, whom she had borne to Jacob, went out to visit the daughters of the land. And when Shechem the son of Hamor the Hivite, the prince of the land, saw her, he took her and lay with her by force.

Genesis 34:1–2

Tragically, Dinah was raped. But she was surrounded by brothers who loved her and were concerned for her welfare. They devised a plan, deceived the Hivites into falling into their trap, and slaughtered all the men in the city. Then they carried off all their wealth and all their women and children (Gen. 34:29).

When Jacob heard what his sons had done to retaliate, he was angry. Apparently not about what had been done to his daughter, or even about the magnitude of their brutal revenge. What Jacob was most concerned about, if you can believe it, was his public relations with the rest of the people in the land.

The second tragedy involved Rachel. While they were still journeying back to the home of Jacob's father, Isaac, God heard Rachel's prayers and gave her another son.

7

> Then they journeyed from Bethel; and when there was still some
> distance to go to Ephrath, Rachel began to give birth and she suffered
> severe labor. And it came about when she was in severe labor that the
> midwife said to her, "Do not fear, for now you have another son." And
> it came about as her soul was departing (for she died), that she named
> him Ben-oni; but his father called him Benjamin. So Rachel died and
> was buried on the way to Ephrath (that is, Bethlehem).
>
> Genesis 35:16–19

What a sad day that must have been! Jacob had worked long and hard
for the woman he loved, and Rachel had waited years to bear his sons.
Now, on the very doorstep of his hometown, with his household and all his
possessions in tow, his children from Leah and his two sons from Rachel,
Jacob's beloved Rachel died at childbirth. On top of that, while he was still
grieving for her,

> Then Israel [Jacob] journeyed on and pitched his tent beyond the
> tower of Eder. And it came about while Israel was dwelling in that
> land, that Reuben went and lay with Bilhah his father's concubine;
> and Israel heard of it.
>   Now there were twelve sons of Jacob—
>
> Genesis 35:21–22

Reuben had sexual relations with Bilhah, who was the mother of
two of his half-brothers. Jacob (Israel) was such a passive father that
when he heard what his son had done, he did absolutely nothing about
it. This seems evident by the fact that the writer, after stating the facts,
just goes on to record the names of Jacob's twelve sons. When he heard
about the rape of his daughter, he did nothing; and when he learned
that his own son had committed incest with Bilhah, again he did nothing. Nothing!

Some might say, "Wait a minute. Maybe Jacob wasn't told about it.
Maybe they kept this information from him." But we know that is not
true; the text says that he heard about both incidents. In fact, when Jacob

was dying, he gathered all of his sons around him and gave them his blessing. "He blessed them, every one with the blessing appropriate to him" (Gen. 49:28). In the course of this, he said:

> "Reuben, you are my first-born;
> My might and the beginning of my strength,
>> Preeminent in dignity and preeminent in power.
> Uncontrolled as water, you shall not have preeminence,
>> Because you went up to your father's bed;
>> Then you defiled it—he went up to my couch."
>
> Genesis 49:3–4

All of this is a poetic way of saying, "Reuben, you are wild and reckless, and you committed a shameful act. Because of this you will no longer excel in honor and power as the firstborn should." A footnote in the New International Version (NIV) states: "Reuben's descendants were characterized by indecision" (see Judges 5:15–16).

If you're like me, when you read this final account, you want to say to Jacob, "Why are you saying all this now, years later? Where were you when all this happened? Why didn't you deal with it at the time, as you should have as a father? Why didn't you step in back then? If you don't, who will guide your children?"

Thanks for staying with me through those historical details. I have gone into all of this background so you will begin to see and understand the deception, the intrigue, the anger, the rebellion, the rivalry, and out-of-control jealousy that were rampant within the ranks of Jacob's boys—all characteristics that had been displayed by their father. This was the home into which young Joseph was born, and it was a pretty pathetic environment in which to raise a boy.

Joseph: The Favorite Son

Keep in mind that from the time of his birth, Joseph was his father's favorite. He was the firstborn of Jacob's favorite wife, Rachel, whom he dearly loved. He was the child of Jacob's old age. Joseph was also unlike his brothers in character and attitude. Perhaps Jacob favored Joseph for all those reasons. Not only did he love him the most, he unwisely showed him great favoritism.

Now, Jacob's other sons were no fools. They might have been lustful, unruly, deceitful, and vengeful, but they weren't stupid. They quickly realized, by the highly visible evidence of their father's indulgences toward Joseph, that he was the pet in the family. His mother had been the favored wife, and Joseph was the favored son. And they weren't about to sit back and let that continue. In only a matter of time, they would unleash their anger. Watch closely as their fuse grew shorter.

> Now Israel [Jacob] loved Joseph more than all his sons, because he was the son of his old age; and he made him a varicolored tunic.
>
> Genesis 37:3

Passive fathers tend to favor the child who is easiest to raise. It's difficult to deal with a child who's hard to raise. (That's why he's hard to raise!) So a passive father will tend to favor the one who isn't difficult. Since Jacob had eleven who were hard to handle, he favored the one who was a delight to his heart.

As I mentioned earlier, Jacob did nothing to hide this favoritism. In fact, he put it on display by giving Joseph "a varicolored tunic," or, as the familiar King James Version translates it, "a coat of many colors." (The New International Version calls it "a richly ornamented robe.")

One reliable Old Testament commentator, H. C. Leupold, says this regarding the style of Joseph's garment: "This tunic was sleeved and extended to the ankles." He draws this conclusion from the Hebrew word *passeem,* which means "wrists" or "ankles."[3]

You can't work very well in a garment that has sleeves and extends all the way down to your ankles, especially if it's a costly, richly ornamented robe. It would be like sending a welder to a construction site wearing a full-length mink coat. In Joseph's day, the working garb was a short, sleeveless tunic. This left the arms and legs free so that workers could easily maneuver and move about. As you can imagine, by giving Joseph this elaborate full-length coat, which was also a sign of nobility in that day, his father was boldly implying, "You can wear this beautiful garment because you don't have to work like those brothers of yours."

A MURDEROUS PLOT

Joseph, when seventeen years of age, was pasturing the flock with his brothers while he was still a youth, along with the sons of Bilhah and the sons of Zilpah, his father's wives. And Joseph brought back a bad report about them to their father. Now Israel loved Joseph more than all his sons, because he was the son of his old age; and he made him a varicolored tunic. And his brothers saw that their father loved him more than all his brothers; and so they hated him and could not speak to him on friendly terms.

Genesis 37:2–4

The home in which Joseph was raised was comprised of a family filled with angry, jealous, and deceitful people. Then, within that hostile environment, for seventeen years, the other sons of Jacob had watched as their father played favorites with Joseph. Their jealousy had turned into resentment and hatred. Don't miss the closing comment. Joseph's brothers had come to despise their younger brother so severely that they could not even speak a kind word to him. Try to imagine the mounting pressure in that home. It was a giant powder keg on the verge of explosion.

Adding insult to injury, Joseph was a dreamer. For whatever reason, he told his brothers about a couple of his dreams. If he hadn't had strained relations before, believe me, the dreams alone would have done the trick.

Then Joseph had a dream, and when he told it to his brothers, they hated him even more. And he said to them, "Please listen to this dream which I have had; for behold, we were binding sheaves in the field, and lo, my sheaf rose up and also stood erect; and behold, your sheaves gathered around and bowed down to my sheaf." Then his brothers said to him, "Are you actually going to reign over us? Or are you really going to rule over us?" So they hated him even more for his dreams and for his words.

Genesis 37:5–8

"Let me tell you about this dream I had," said Joseph.

And when they had heard him out, his brothers sneered, "What? Do you really think you are going to be our master, that *we* are going serve *you?*" We can imagine each one thinking *Get a life, Joe!*

And Joseph said, "Wait, I'm not through. I had another dream also." The biblical text states:

> Now he had still another dream, and related it to his brothers, and said, "Lo, I have had still another dream; and behold, the sun and the moon and eleven stars were bowing down to me." And he related it to his father and to his brothers; and his father rebuked him and said to him, "What is this dream that you have had? Shall I and your mother and your brothers actually come to bow ourselves down before you to the ground?" And his brothers were jealous of him, but his father kept the saying in mind.

Genesis 37:9–11

When his dad heard about this dream, he must have frowned as he said, in effect, "Wait a minute, Son. What's this all about? Are you trying to tell us that I'm the sun, your mother is the moon, your brothers are the eleven stars, and we're all bowing down to you? Now *I'm* a little concerned about you, Joseph."

Once again, Jacob responded passively. He noticed what Joseph said—and even got the point—but he didn't seem to see beyond it. I'm not sure he noticed the jealousy of his other sons; or if he did, he didn't deal with it. He backed away, saying in essence, "Well, that's just the way it is. That's just the way we are in this family." Parental passivity is lethal in a family that's getting out of control. And here's a classic example. The fuse has just about reached the keg.

Sent by His Father

Sometime after this, Joseph's "brothers went to pasture their father's flocks," but Joseph didn't go with them, possibly because Jacob wanted to keep him by his side.

> Then his brothers went to pasture their father's flock in Shechem. And Israel said to Joseph, "Are not your brothers pasturing the flock in Shechem? Come, and I will send you to them." And he said to him, "I will go." Then he said to him, "Go now and see about the welfare of your brothers and the welfare of the flock; and bring word back to me." So he sent him from the valley of Hebron, and he came to Shechem.
>
> Genesis 37:12–14

It's interesting to note that Jacob's sons returned to the area called Shechem to pasture their animals. This was the very place where their sister, Dinah, had been raped and where they had killed all the men and raided their homes and property. When Jacob realized where they had gone, he probably thought, "Because of what they did to the people of Shechem, my boys may be in danger." So he ordered Joseph to go and check on his brothers and report back.

One wonders what Jacob was thinking at this point. Or if he was thinking at all. Was he totally oblivious to the situation? How could he avoid seeing the seething hatred and jealousy within his own household? Had he no concept of the danger into which he was sending his favorite son? In reality, he set Joseph up for what happened. You're about to witness an explosion of pent-up emotions.

> . . . So Joseph went after his brothers and found them at Dothan. When they saw him from a distance and before he came close to them, they plotted against him to put him to death. And they said to one another, "Here comes this dreamer! Now then, come and let us kill him and throw him into one of the pits; and we will say, 'A wild beast devoured him.' Then let us see what will become of his dreams!"
>
> Genesis 37:17–20

Mistreated by His Brothers

You talk about hostility in a family! As soon as they saw Joseph coming, the brothers' immediate reaction was stated with clinched teeth: "It's the dreamer! Let's kill him!" This is a timely moment to point out that the mixture of a passive parent in a hostile family environment results in out-of-control consequences. By now, the brothers had murder on their minds.

Interestingly, at that point, Reuben steps in.

> But Reuben heard this and rescued him out of their hands and said, "Let us not take his life." Reuben further said to them, "Shed no blood. Throw him into this pit that is in the wilderness, but do not lay hands on him"—that he might rescue him out of their hands, to restore him to his father.
>
> Genesis 37:21–22

Remember Reuben? This is Reuben, the firstborn. This is Reuben, who had slept with his father's concubine. Perhaps because he was the eldest, he felt some sense of responsibility for his younger brother. Or in an unguarded moment he was becoming a better man than he had been.

"Look, let's not kill him," Reuben said. "Let's just throw him in a pit and leave him. We might teach him a lesson, but there's no reason to kill him." Meanwhile, Reuben was thinking that he would return later, rescue Joseph, and take him back home.

> So it came about, when Joseph reached his brothers, that they stripped Joseph of his tunic, the varicolored tunic that was on him; and they took him and threw him into the pit. Now the pit was empty, without any water in it.
>
> Then they sat down to eat a meal. . . .
>
> Genesis 37:23–25

Obviously the brothers must have agreed with Reuben's plan. But notice the first thing they did when Joseph arrived: "They stripped Joseph of his tunic." That hated robe of special favoritism was the first thing to go.

"Remove that robe," they said. It was as if they were saying: "Take off that fur coat! You're no better than we are." Then they threw him into the pit. After that, they sat down and had lunch! All their anger has made them ravenous. Amazing, isn't it? No guilty conscience here!

A CARAVAN TO EGYPT

Then they sat down to eat a meal. And as they raised their eyes and looked, behold, a caravan of Ishmaelites was coming from Gilead, with their camels bearing aromatic gum and balm and myrrh, on their way to bring them down to Egypt. And Judah said to his brothers, "What profit is it for us to kill our brother and cover up his blood? "Come and let us sell him to the Ishmaelites and not lay our hands on him; for he is our brother, our own flesh." And his brothers listened to him. Then some Midianite traders passed by, so they pulled him up and lifted Joseph out of the pit, and sold him to the Ishmaelites for twenty shekels of silver. Thus they brought Joseph into Egypt.

Genesis 37:25–28

A chill runs up my spine when I read what these men did to their own brother. Spotting a caravan of traders, Judah said, in effect, "Hey, Reuben's right. Let's not kill the kid. After all, he is a member of our family, and we don't need his blood on our hands. Let's dump him. Better yet, let's make some money in the process." The others agreed, and for 20 pieces of silver (which is what they would have paid for a handicapped slave in those days) they turned him over to a group of total strangers—a band of Midianite traders.

So they took Joseph's tunic, and slaughtered a male goat, and dipped the tunic in the blood; and they sent the varicolored tunic and brought it to their father and said, "We found this; please examine it to see whether it is your son's tunic or not." Then he examined it and said, "It is my son's tunic. A wild beast has devoured him; Joseph has surely been torn to pieces!"

Genesis 37:31–33

As the caravan wended its way across the fields and out of sight, the brothers calmly dipped Joseph's robe in the blood of a freshly killed goat. Then they took the bloodstained garment back to their father, tossed it on the floor, and said, "We found this. We think it may be your son's robe."

When he saw the bloody evidence, Jacob came to the desired conclusion: His beloved son, Joseph, was dead.

Just one more deception, one more act of hatred in a family filled with both. What a harsh reality! What tragic consequences. Jacob, an aging father, had sowed the wind and was now reaping the whirlwind. I cannot help but wonder what went through Jacob's mind that night as he, alone, tossed and turned through those torturous hours. I wonder if he might have realized his own failure as a father, and poured out his heart in anguished prayer.

LESSONS LEARNED FROM ADVERSITY

Perhaps this is a good time to call to mind several lessons we can learn from Jacob's family and Joseph's adversity. The first is obvious.

- *No enemy is more subtle than passivity.* When parents are passive, they may eventually discipline, but by then the delayed reaction is often carried out in anger. Passivity waits and waits until finally, when it can wait no longer, it comes down with both feet! When that happens, children are not disciplined, they are brutalized. Passivity not only blinds us to the here and now, it makes us inconsistent.

I'm extremely exercised in my soul these days on behalf of the American family. And if Christians don't begin to wake up and take control of the situation, through the power of the Lord Jesus Christ, who in the world will?

Now, you may say, "Well, I'm a grandparent now. My child-rearing days are over." Or, "I'm single. What can I do about it?" But those statements are cop-outs, convenient excuses. We are all born into families, we all live in families of one kind or another, and we all interact with families every day of our lives. In case you haven't noticed lately, the family is on a slippery slope, scarcely resembling the family of fifty years ago.

I was shocked recently to see a chart that compared the top disciplinary problems of 1990 with those of 1940, based on the testimony of public school teachers.

1940	1990
Talking out of turn	Drug abuse
Chewing gum	Alcohol abuse
Making noise	Pregnancy
Running in the halls	Suicide
Cutting in line	Rape
Dress code infractions	Robbery
Littering	Assault

Since 1940 the top disciplinary problems in public schools have taken a downward plunge from chewing gum and cutting in line to drug and alcohol abuse, rape, and assault.[4]

My shock turned to dismay while reading Stephen Covey's latest book, *The Seven Habits of Highly Effective Families.* In a penetrating chapter devoted to parents who desire to make a difference in a world that's lost its way, Covey tells the story of a seven-year-old boy who was troubled. His father, thinking he may be having nightmares, urged him to tell him what was bothering him. After a lot of persuasion, the boy began to describe several scenes of horrible, hard-core pornography. Restraining his surprise, the dad probed to find out where his son had been exposed to such filth. The final finger pointed to a nine-year-old boy in the neighborhood, who had turned a computer room in his basement into a porn shop—and neither of his parents knew anything about it.

Covey asks, How could this happen? How could it be that we live in a society where technology makes it possible for children—who have no wisdom or experience or judgment on these matters—to become victims of such sick, deeply addictive mental poisoning as pornography?

Over the past thirty years the situation for families has changed powerfully and dramatically.

- Illegitimate birthrates have increased more than 400 percent.

- The percentage of families headed by a single parent has more than tripled.

- The divorce rate has more than doubled.

- Teenage suicide has increased almost 300 percent.

- Scholastic Aptitude Test scores among all students have dropped 73 points.

- The number-one health problem for American women today is domestic violence. Four million women are beaten each year by their partners.

- One-fourth of all adolescents contract a sexually transmitted disease before they graduate from high school.[5]

None of this should surprise us, not really. After all, the average child spends seven hours a day watching television but only five minutes a day with Dad.[6]

You may be wondering how all this ties in with the story of Joseph. Frankly, quite well, since the family of Jacob found themselves in the backwash of a father who seemed to fold his arms and look the other way.

Never, ever forget these four words:

Passivity is an enemy!

There's a second lesson we learn from Joseph's teenage struggles.

- *No response is more cruel than jealousy.* Solomon was right when he said, "Jealousy is cruel as the grave" (Song of Solomon 8:6, RSV). Jealousy, if allowed to grow and fester, leads to devastating consequences. If you allow jealousy to rage within your family or between your children, you are asking for trouble. At some point, it will manifest itself in detrimental ways.

We have to deal with attitudes as severely as we deal with actions. Christian parents, learn that! Come down hard on wrong attitudes! But when you catch those beautiful glimpses of right attitudes, reward! Build up! Of course, in order to do that, and to be a consistent role model, your own attitudes must be right.

Jacob and Rachel, Leah and Laban, quite candidly, set some very poor examples for the rest of the family. In Joseph's early life we can clearly see the effect of a passive father, an absent mother, a family filled with deceit and jealousy and infighting, children left on their own to figure out life for themselves, and the sin and mistreatment that crept in and was, in fact, tolerated. Jealousy never corrects itself; it only leads to greater ills.

Enough of the negatives. Let's find in all this at least one magnificent lesson of hope: *No action is more powerful than prayer.* I realize that the biblical story does not state that Jacob turned to God in prayer, but surely, he could have done so! How else could he have gone on with his life? Where else could he have turned for hope?

The same could be said for you and me. Prayer brings power to endure. Those who are older are a source of wisdom for young parents and for children and grandchildren. Single men and women also have much to offer, whether within their own extended families or within the family of the church. Broken, hollow lives can find new strength to recover. It's at this point I would say that Joseph, without question, turned his situation over to God, even as the caravan made its way toward Egypt. Surely he knew, even at seventeen, that his only hope would come through God's faithful intervention! Surely, he cried out to the One who, alone, was in sovereign control of his future! And, surely, must we!

We leave Joseph in a most precarious set of circumstances. Abandoned by his brothers and left at the mercy of careless mercenaries en route to a destination totally unfamiliar to him, the teenage son of Jacob had nowhere to look but up. I am convinced he did just that. Rather than lick his wounds and vow someday to take revenge, the boy must have determined in his heart, like Daniel who would one day follow his model, not to defile himself with wicked and self-defeating plans to get even. Though unable to send a final message to his aging father, he knew his Lord was aware of his situation and was ready to hear his plea for mercy. Surely he called upon Him!

F. B. Meyer agrees. With tender heart for this lonely lad, he writes:

> How eager his desire to send just one last message to his father! And with all these thoughts, there would mingle a wondering thought of the great God whom he had learned to worship. What would He say to this? Little did he think then that hereafter he should look back on that day as one of the most gracious links in a chain of loving providences; or that he should ever say, "Be not grieved, nor angry with yourselves: God did send me here before you." It is very sweet, as life passes by, to be able to look back on dark and mysterious events, and to trace the hand of God where we once saw only the malice and cruelty of man.[7]

Joseph has only begun to experience life's "dark and mysterious events." But through all of them the hand of God will hold him close and ultimately trace His sovereign plan.

CHAPTER TWO

Resisting Temptation

On April 9, 1945, Dietrich Bonhoeffer was executed by the Nazis. He was only thirty-nine years old. Yet in those thirty-nine years, Bonhoeffer had distinguished himself as a pastor and theologian as well as an active and courageous member of the resistance against Hitler's Third Reich. He was loved by many back then in his native Germany, but now, even more so, by the family of God around the world. His works on spirituality are still widely read today, and *The Cost of Discipleship, Life Together, Ethics,* and *Letters and Papers from Prison* are considered classics. But the best, in my opinion, is a small booklet fewer than fifty pages long titled, *Temptation.* In this brief treatise, Bonhoeffer has left us with the single most descriptive explanation of temptation anywhere outside the Bible.

In our members there is a slumbering inclination towards desire which is both sudden and fierce. With irresistible power desire seizes mastery over the flesh. All at once a secret, smouldering fire is kindled. The flesh burns and is in flames. It makes no difference whether it is sexual desire, or ambition, or vanity, or desire for revenge, or love of fame and power, or greed for money, or, finally, that strange desire for the beauty of the world, of nature. Joy in God is in course of being extinguished in us and we seek all our joy in the creature. At this moment God is quite unreal to us, he loses all reality, and only desire for the creature is real; the only reality is the devil. Satan does not here fill us with hatred of God, but with forgetfulness of God. . . . The lust thus aroused envelops the mind and will of man in deepest darkness. The powers of clear discrimination and of decision are taken from us. . . . It is here that everything within me rises up against the Word of God.[1]

There is not a person who has cast his shadow across this earth, including Jesus Christ, who has not faced temptation. And there is not a single person who has ever lived, except Christ, who has not yielded to it at one time or another and suffered the consequences. Temptation is an inevitable part of our fallen world. We cannot escape it.

Temptation also wears many faces. There is, for example, *material temptation,* which is the lust for things. It might be as big as a house or as small as a ring. It might be as bright and dazzling as a brand-new Porsche or as dull and dusty as an antique roll-top desk. Yet, who hasn't felt the burning passion of lust for things? And who hasn't at times yielded to it unwisely?

Then there is what we will call *personal temptation,* which is the lust for fame, for authority, for power, or control over others. It might be as simple as lust for a title like "CEO" or "president" or "doctor" or "professor" or "admiral." There is nothing wrong with those titles or those positions, until lust comes and says, "You deserve that, for what it will mean to *you.* "

Finally, there is *sensual temptation,* which is lust for another person—or, in reality, lust for the person's body. I'm referring here to the hedonistic desire to have and enjoy that which is not one's own, either legally or morally.

Because Joseph engaged in battle with this third category of temptation, we shall limit our thoughts in this chapter to that particular one. As we do, let's not forget Bonhoeffer's very practical reminder that when we yield to that particular temptation, "the powers of clear discrimination and of decision are taken from us."

Before we look at his temptation, though, we need to see exactly what has been happening to Joseph since we left him, in the last chapter, among a band of Midianites on a slow-moving caravan to Egypt.

THE HISTORIC SETTING

Jacob had accepted the fact that his son, Joseph, was dead. To his brothers, at least as much as they would admit to themselves, he was gone for good, perhaps even dead by now. But in reality, Joseph was very much alive.

> Now Joseph had been taken down to Egypt; and Potiphar, an Egyptian officer of Pharaoh, the captain of the bodyguard, bought him from the Ishmaelites, who had taken him down there.
>
> Genesis 39:1

Joseph found himself in a country and culture he didn't know, surrounded by a language he didn't understand. This once-longed-for child of Rachel and openly favored son of Jacob had been sold as a common slave, and forced into a situation that seemed even worse than the pit into which his brothers had initially thrown him.

As we are introduced to his circumstances in Egypt, notice that two things are conspicuous by their absence. First, there is no mention of time. We have no indication of how long Joseph has been in Potiphar's house when these events begin to unfold. He could have been there two years or two months.

Second, nothing is said about the adjustments that Joseph had to make. Remember, he had come from a rural culture, an unsophisticated people, and a home where he had been the pride and joy of his mother and the favorite child of a doting, aging father.

Without warning, he was grabbed roughly by his brothers, stripped of his beautiful robe, and dumped into a deep, dirty pit. He was rescued from that situation, only to be sold to hardened slave traders and taken overland by caravan to a distant land, where he was set on the block and sold like a cheap piece of merchandise. The changes and adjustments that he faced must have been phenomenal.

We read in the Genesis account that he was sold to a man named Potiphar, who is described as the "captain of the bodyguard" or, as the NIV translates it, "captain of the guard." This group was an elite, courageous band of rugged men. The Jewish historian Alfred Edersheim describes that group by telling us that Potiphar was the "chief of the executioners." No matter what title you give him, Potiphar was nobody to fool around with; he was a man of seasoned military experience with power over life and death. Yet Joseph not only adjusted to his new situation, but flourished in it—and for one major reason. That reason emerges in a beautiful phrase that appears a number of times in Joseph's story: "And the LORD was with Joseph."

> And the LORD was with Joseph, so he became a successful man. And he was in the house of his master, the Egyptian. Now his master saw that the LORD was with him and how the LORD caused all that he did to prosper in his hand. So Joseph found favor in his sight, and became his personal servant; and he made him overseer over his house, and all that he owned he put in his charge. And it came about that from the time he made him overseer in his house, and over all that he owned, the LORD blessed the Egyptian's house on account of Joseph; thus the LORD's blessing was upon all that he owned, in the house and in the field. So he left everything he owned in Joseph's charge; and with him there he did not concern himself with anything except the food which he ate. Now Joseph was handsome in form and appearance.
>
> Genesis 39:2–6

The sovereign God of Israel was intimately involved in Joseph's life. He guided him. He gave him facility in the Egyptian language. On top of all that, he gave him favor in the eyes of Potiphar. Clearly, God was the secret of Joseph's success. Luck had nothing to do with it.

Furthermore, Joseph didn't have to tell Potiphar that the Lord was with him; Potiphar could see it for himself. "Now his master saw that the LORD was with him" (v. 3). Furthermore, Joseph didn't use his spirituality as a manipulative tool to get benefits from his boss. Simply because the Lord caused all that Joseph did to prosper, Joseph found favor in his sight. Notice, it doesn't say that Joseph *asked* favors from Potiphar; he found favor with Potiphar.

Joseph's faith in Jehovah was recognized by Potiphar because he saw the evidence of the outworking of that faith in Joseph's life and labor—a winning combination. Joseph was a hard-working, diligent young man. So much so that Potiphar increased his responsibilities and his authority. Ultimately, the captain of the guard put him in charge of his own household. In other words, he put all that he possessed under Joseph's jurisdiction. The Hebrew says, "All that came to him he put in his charge." Interesting. Not only the things that Potiphar owned, but all of the benefits that he accrued finally wound up under the watchful eye and guiding hand of Joseph. What a tremendous promotion—from a common slave, probably one among dozens of slaves in Potiphar's home, to running the household of the top military man in Egypt. But it gets even better, for through Joseph the Lord blessed Potiphar's house and all that he owned.

With greater success comes greater measures of trust, which, by the way, lead to greater times of unguarded vulnerability. Regarding the latter, F. B. Meyer writes insightfully,

> We may expect temptation in the days of prosperity and ease rather than in those of privation and toil. Not on the glacier slopes of the Alps, but in the sunny plains of the Campagna; not when the youth is climbing arduously the steep ladder of fame, but when he has entered the golden portals; not where men frown, but where they smile sweet exquisite smiles of flattery—it is *there*, it is *there*, that the temptress lies in wait! Beware![2]

What a wise exhortation! This warning is not of concern to the person who is down and out. This message is addressed to the successful, to the up-and-coming executive, to the man or woman on the way to the top of the heap, to the individual who is experiencing the benefits and favor of God, who is reaping the benefits of increased privacy and trust. Thomas Carlyle, the Scottish essayist, was right when he said, "Adversity is sometimes hard upon a man, but for one man who can stand prosperity, there are a hundred that will stand adversity."[3] The temptations that accompany prosperity are far greater (and far more subtle) than those that accompany adversity.

Joseph was certainly prospering. Potiphar left everything in his charge and we read, "he [Potiphar] did not concern himself with anything except the food which he ate." Now that's trust!

Here was a slave who had earned the right to be respected and trusted. As a result Potiphar turned everything over to him. I take this to mean that Joseph determined his own schedule, that he organized all of Potiphar's estate and administered all his finances. Potiphar placed everything in Joseph's hands.

But remember, with greater success come greater measures of trust, which lead inevitably to greater times of vulnerability. At such junctures "we may expect temptation in the days of prosperity . . . it is *there* that the temptress lies in wait! Beware!"

The Spirit of God, who hovered over the writing of the biblical text, led to the selecting of words wisely and accurately chosen. Thus Genesis 39:6 closes with a somewhat surprising yet significant sentence: "Now Joseph was handsome in form and appearance." The Living Bible says, "Joseph, by the way, was a very handsome young man." The New International Version reads, "Joseph was well-built and handsome." These words used to describe Joseph's appearance are found only four times in the Old Testament: with Joseph, with Saul, with David, and with Absalom.

Now understand that there is nothing wrong with being physically well-built or handsome. But with these attributes come unique temptations. Here was a man who had just about everything—fame and power, authority and respect. Here was a house servant who had it made—his own private quarters, access to very confidential information, and the complete trust of his employer. On top of all that he was a good-looking man who, without interest in doing so, caught the eye of women. Not surprisingly it was on those physical attributes that the enemy of Joseph's soul, the tempter, concentrated.

The Scriptures waste no words. Nor did Potiphar's wife.

> And it came about after these events that his master's wife looked with desire at Joseph, and she said, "Lie with me."
>
> Genesis 39:7

That's what I would call *the direct approach!* Let's return to an earlier comment. Greater success leads to greater times of vulnerability. It is *there* that the temptress lies in wait! Beware! The writer of Genesis states, "And it came about after these events," referring to the previous verses telling of Joseph's success. Joseph was ripe for this attack from the enemy; therefore, the attack struck with laserlike accuracy.

Potiphar's wife was brazenly and shamelessly aggressive: "Come to bed with me. Let's have sex." Most others then and now would have been caught off guard and at least momentarily felt flattered by such a seductive statement. Not Joseph. Nor even for a moment. Without hesitation and being absolutely secure in himself and his God, he responded with equal boldness.

> But he refused and said to his master's wife, "Behold, with me here, my master does not concern himself with anything in the house, and he has put all that he owns in my charge. There is no one greater in this house than I, and he has withheld nothing from me except you, because you are his wife. How then could I do this great evil, and sin against God?"
>
> Genesis 39:8–9

Verse 8 states simply, "He refused." Joseph refused. If you forget everything else I've written thus far, don't forget those two wonderful words. If you're sitting there thinking that Joseph was some kind of spiritual giant, put it out of your mind. If you're thinking that some supernatural cloud of protection held him in check, forget it. Just look at the evidence. Here was an Egyptian woman offering her body and a young Jewish servant being tempted by her bold advances. And so? "He refused." He said NO! He resisted her alluring words; he stared her down, determined not to yield.

How could he do that? Two reasons. First, his loyalty to his master. He said to this woman, "My master trusts me. He has given me responsibility for everything he owns. The only thing that is not mine is you—his wife. I could never betray his trust."

And the second reason was his loyalty to God. He said, "How could I do this great evil, and sin against God?"

Clarence Edward Macartney adds a touch of realism:

> This was no ordinary temptation. Joseph was not a stone, a mummy, but a red-blooded young man in his late twenties. It was not one temptation on one day, but a repeated temptation. . . . An old story tells how when Joseph began to talk about God to the temptress, she flung her skirt over the bust of the god that stood in the chamber and said, "Now, God will not see." But Joseph answered, "My God sees!"[4]

How could this "red-blooded young man in his late twenties" say no? Because he knew his life was an open book before his God. By now in his life Joseph's God had become more real to him than anything or anyone else on earth. He was in a private chamber, perfectly safe with the master's wife, who had set him up for this desired moment of lustful pleasure. He was a handsome young bachelor. They were alone. It would have been the most natural thing in the world to yield. But Joseph said that this is a great evil, a heinous sin against his God. And so he walked away.

You may be thinking *Whew! boy, I am glad that's over and done with. I thank God for Joseph's example. You strongly resist temptation like that, and it's out of your life forever.* You wish! Read on:

> And it came about as she spoke to Joseph day after day, that he did not listen to her to lie beside her, or be with her.
>
> Genesis 39:10

Potiphar's wife refused to take no for an answer. She wasn't about to be ignored, so she pressed Joseph day after day after day. This was an evil seductress. She was driven to have sex with Joseph. All his talk about those noble reasons for resisting only intensified her determination. She cared nothing about the sanctity of her marriage or the trust between her husband and this young man. She was interested in gratifying her sensual desires—*now.*

If you're living in the imaginary bubble that somehow temptation, once resisted, will vanish, burst it this very moment. As a matter of fact, when you think like this, you become an even greater target for the tempter. Furthermore, it helps to keep in mind that the tempter wants the respected person, the person who is quoted by others, the successful individual, the trusted partner, the godly soul.

That's why it's not surprising Potiphar's wife went after Joseph with such relentless persistence. He was a catch! Get him, and she'd conquered something! But Joseph refused to budge. And aren't we glad he did! The slightest hint of interest in her would have spelled his doom.

Bonhoeffer's words are worth repeating:

> In our members there is a slumbering inclination towards desire which is both sudden and fierce. With irresistible power desire seizes mastery over the flesh. All at once a secret, smouldering fire is kindled. . . . The lust thus aroused envelops the mind and will of man in deepest darkness. The powers of clear discrimination and of decision are taken from us.[5]

Once the embers of lust begin to smolder, the vivid scene portrayed in James 1 goes into action.

> Let no one say when he is tempted, "I am being tempted by God"; for God cannot be tempted by evil, and He Himself does not tempt any one. But each one is tempted when he is carried away and enticed by his own lust.
>
> James 1:13–14

The appeal of sensual lust works like a magnet, drawing two "sudden and fierce" forces toward each other—inner desire and an outer bait. Let's face it, you can't escape the bait if you live in the real world. In fact, even if you somehow manage to shut yourself away from the real world, your mind will not let you escape the outer bait. But keep in mind that there is no sin in the bait. The sin is in the bite. When the lust of another tempts you to give in to *your own* lust, so much so that your resistance weakens, you have been enticed. You have given in to the lure of temptation. The secret is modeled beautifully by Joseph. He refused to weaken. He continued to resist.

Potiphar's wife dropped the bait day after day after day. And each time Joseph refused to take it. "No, no, no!" he replied. Not only did he not listen to her, it got to where he did not even want to be near her. She was not safe to be around.

Joseph had rebuffed her time and time again, refusing to yield to her advances. Finally, she set a trap for him.

> Now it happened one day that he went into the house to do his work, and none of the men of the household was there inside. And she caught him by his garment, saying, "Lie with me!" And he left his garment in her hand and fled, and went outside.
>
> Genesis 39:11–12

Joseph had come into the house to do his work one day. He noticed the house was quiet. There were no servants about. Who knows why? Perhaps Potiphar's wife had sent them on errands to get them out of the way. Whatever the reason, she was alone with Joseph in the house, and she again made her move. Only this time she would not take no for an answer. She went beyond verbal advances and physically grabbed hold of Joseph. She held on so tightly that when he jerked away from her and dashed out into the street, he left his outer robe in her hands.

What a clear image! What a practical spotlight on truth from Joseph's life. What strong biblical counsel. Whenever the New Testament lingers on the subject of sensual temptation, it gives us one command: RUN! The Bible does not tell us to reason with it. It does not tell us to think about it and claim verses. It tells us to FLEE! I have discovered you cannot yield to sensuality if you're running away from it. So? Run for your life! Get out of there! If you try to reason with lust or play around with sensual thoughts, you will finally yield. You can't fight it. That's why the Spirit of God forcefully commands, "Run!"

And that's exactly what Joseph did. He ran out into the street, and Potiphar's wife was left standing there, again rejected, with his garment in her hands. She was enraged.

William Congreve's familiar words turned to reality: "Heaven has no rage like love to hatred turned, nor hell a fury like a woman scorned."[6]

Every ounce of Mrs. Potiphar's lust turned to fury. Having lusted after him, she now despised him—which resulted in a trumped-up accusation of rape.

> When she saw that he had left his garment in her hand, and had fled outside, she called to the men of her household, and said to them, "See, he has brought in a Hebrew to us to make sport of us; he came in to me to lie with me, and I screamed."
>
> Genesis 39:13–14

Now, this scorned woman wanted only revenge. To accomplish this, she built a false case against Joseph, using a piece of circumstantial evidence—his robe.

> So she left his garment beside her until his master came home. Then she spoke to him with these words, "The Hebrew slave, whom you brought to us, came in to me to make sport of me; and it happened as I raised my voice and screamed, that he left his garment beside me and fled outside."
>
> Now it came about when his master heard the words of his wife, which she spoke to him, saying, "This is what your slave did to me," that his anger burned. So Joseph's master took him and put him into the jail, the place where the king's prisoners were confined; and he was there in the jail.
>
> Genesis 39:16–20

She called the men of the household and lied, saying, "This Jew my husband brought into our Egyptian home . . . look at what he's done. He tried to lie with me and I screamed! And here's the evidence. His robe. I grabbed it when he attacked me." I'm sure she did scream, but it was a scream of rage, not a scream of rape. Her screams and tears were screams and tears of a scorned woman who was enraged that handsome young Joseph had resisted her advances, that he wanted nothing to do with her.

I read the words from the biblical account, and my heart goes out to Joseph. I think, *Oh, if there's ever a time to reward this man Joseph, reward him now, God! Reward him for saying no day after day after day! Reward him for running instead of yielding!* But God is not through with His man, Joseph. God is not like us. He patiently and faithfully works in ways we would never employ. God sees far beyond this situation and knows what needs to be done deep within the recesses of Joseph's life as He prepares him for greatness in the years ahead. Therefore, He remains silent even though Joseph was caught in a trap of circumstantial evidence. Watch closely as the plot against Joseph unfolds. On the surface, it is heartbreaking.

THE PERSONAL RAMIFICATIONS

Joseph was absolutely innocent, but the circumstances were against him. Potiphar's wife had both his robe as evidence and her position in the household as manipulative power. She used both against him, which landed him in jail.

Now I don't want to be guilty of reading something into this story that isn't true, but I think there is evidence here to support the idea that Potiphar did not totally believe his wife. After all, he was the captain of the bodyguard and chief executioner. If he believed a slave had attempted to rape his wife, do you think he would simply have put him into prison? I think he would have killed him on the spot. Ancient Egypt was not exactly easy on crime.

Instead of having him tortured or put to death, however, Potiphar had Joseph put "into the jail, the place where the king's prisoners were confined." Seems to me Potiphar was mainly angry at having lost his best servant due to a wife he knew to be unfaithful. Be that as it may, Joseph still wound up behind bars.

Imagine what must have been going through Joseph's mind at this point, shortly after he was incarcerated. He was not only innocent, he had resisted blatant temptation over and over again. (He'd never read Genesis 41. He didn't know what the final outcome would be. He didn't know that in a matter of years he would be prime minister of Egypt.) All the man knew at this painful moment was that he had done what was right and had suffered wrong for it. Time dragged by. Days turned into months. He was, again, unfairly rejected—forgotten—totally helpless.

But somehow, in the midst of this unfair situation, Joseph sensed that Jehovah's hand was in all this. "Joseph, you're Mine. Just wait. I'm with you. I'm not ignoring you or rejecting you. You will be a better man, Joseph, because of this accusation against you. I'm not through preparing you for My service."

Does that sound too pious? Are those meanderings too much for you to swallow? Am I off base here? Not if we believe the rest of the story recorded in this chapter.

> But the LORD was with Joseph and extended kindness to him, and gave him favor in the sight of the chief jailer. And the chief jailer committed to Joseph's charge all the prisoners who were in the jail; so that whatever was done there, he was responsible for it. The chief jailer did not supervise anything under Joseph's charge because the LORD was with him; and whatever he did, the LORD made to prosper.
>
> Genesis 39:21–23

Did you notice that key phrase? ". . . the Lord was with him." The Lord's hand was on Joseph. But the relationship was reciprocal. Joseph also obeyed his God. Instead of being bitter and angry, he served God above all else. As a result, he prospered—*even in prison.* Amazing!

A FEW PRACTICAL WORDS OF HOPE

It may be that you are facing temptation right now. Perhaps you have already yielded. A few of my readers may be thinking, *Preach it, brother, I need to hear it. So far I've resisted the lure of sensual temptation, and I need help to keep standing strong.* But not one person reading this can say, "I don't know what you're talking about, Chuck. I've never encountered anything like this in my entire life."

And so, for all who read these lines, let me close this chapter with some practical advice. These are principles that have worked for me, by the grace of God. If you plan to resist temptation, you must meet four requirements. I'll cut to the chase, then spell each one out.

1. You must not be weakened by your situation.

2. You must not be deceived by the persuasion.

3. You must not be gentle with your emotions.

4. You must not be confused with the immediate results.

When it came to his situation, Joseph had it made. Economically, he was secure. Vocationally, he was respected and trusted. Personally, he was handsome and charming. He could have allowed all of this to weaken his resolve, to give in to the opportunity offered him, but he did not.

I repeat the warning: If you plan to resist temptation, you must not be weakened by your situation. This is in keeping with the second requirement to which you must hold fast: You must not be deceived by the persuasion. Your temptress or tempter will have just the right words and will be very persuasive:

- "My husband doesn't meet my needs like you could."

- "By doing this, you'll prove that you really care for me."

- "Who will ever find out? We're completely alone, absolutely safe."

- "Look, we're going to be married soon anyway. Why wait? What does it matter?"

- "I'm so terribly lonely. God understands—that's why He brought you into my life."

- "Just this once. Never, never, never again."

- "What's grace all about if it won't cover something as natural as this?"

You and I need to discern the times in which we live. We are living in an era that attempts to stretch grace to heretical extremes. I see it and hear it virtually every week of my life. So allow me to say this very straight: The greatest gift you can give to your marriage partner is your purity, your fidelity. The greatest character trait you can provide your spouse and your family is moral and ethical self-control. Stand firm, my friend. Refuse to yield. Joseph did and so can you. So *must* you!

Deceptive baits are set out about us each day, and they don't all come from individuals. Some of them come from a cable television channel or the Internet or a magazine or peer pressure at school or colleagues at work. You'll hear Mrs. Potiphar's persuasive words over and over again. You'll feel like a prude, the only one around who's not yielding. Don't be deceived by the persuasion no matter how beautiful and appealing the words may sound. It is a lie. Remember, it is all a lie.

Third, let me underscore this principle, especially: You must not be gentle with your emotions. Yes, you read that correctly. Your inner feelings will plead for satisfaction. Temptation will work on them, begging for understanding. Remember how rugged Joseph was with his? Verse 8, "He refused!" Verse 9, he called her temptation "this great evil, and a sin against God." Verse 10 tells us that he didn't even listen to her or linger in her presence. Verse 12 states that he fled from her! If you need to, press it to the extreme, get downright RUDE about it, if necessary.

I can hear someone respond to this: "Well, I don't know about that. I thought the Christian message was love." Love of evil? Love of lust? *Get real!*

The late Dag Hammarskjold once wrote:

> You cannot play with the animal in you without becoming wholly animal, play with falsehood without forfeiting your right to truth, play with cruelty without losing your sensitivity of mind. He who wants to keep his garden tidy doesn't reserve a plot for weeds."[7]

Fourth, and finally, you must not be confused by the immediate results. Again, remember Joseph. After doing what was right and resisting evil, he was falsely accused and dumped in prison. And if you take the time to read ahead, you'll see that he was later forgotten for an extended period of time.

Don't be confused by the immediate results. You may lose your job. You may lose your lover (if you want to call that person a lover). You may lose acceptance by the group. You may be ridiculed. You may be bumped out of the club. You may be the only one who's not "doing it." Then be the only one! If you name the name of Jesus Christ, name it fully, name it completely, and keep yourself morally clean from this day forward. Even if it means demotion or loss of stature or loss of a job. Get out! You owe it to your character and to your family. Most of all, you owe it to your God.

The truth evidenced in Joseph's life is for all of us—married or unmarried, divorced or remarried, man or woman, young or old. Whatever your situation, no matter how alluring or pleasurable or momentarily delightful the bait looks, don't linger. Claim the supernatural strength that comes from knowing Jesus Christ and, operating under the control of His power, stand strong in His might. Right now, this very moment, determine to be a Joseph. Make up your mind to join his ranks—and from this day forward, *resist*.

Otherwise, *you will yield*. It's only a matter of time.

CHAPTER THREE

Imprisoned and Forgotten

Victim. That's a word we hear a lot these days.

I realize some rush to the word too quickly and too often. There are those who claim they've been victimized, regardless of the whole truth of their story. If their parents were a little too strict on occasion, they claim they were victims of child abuse. If the boss expected extra effort and needed them to work overtime to get a project done, they felt victimized by a tyrannical authority figure. I'm not referring to such nonsense here.

I'm talking about genuinely being victims of unfair and unjust mistreatment. Periodically we read of such people and our hearts go out to them. Children mistreat other children. Students in school mistreat other students. Wives mistreat their husbands; and husbands, their wives. Pastors mistreat their congregations and vice versa. Our mailbag at Insight for Living often includes letters from broken or angry victims of extreme mistreatment. As we read their stories and try to respond in ways that will help, our hearts are touched by the pain people live with. How often I've thought: *It just isn't fair! That person did what was right, but was treated so wrong. Why Lord?*

There are stories of people who have been severely abused. A wife has been abandoned or abused, a child has been neglected or molested. A husband has been left suddenly, without warning, by a wife who wants to go her own way and doesn't want her family anymore. Individuals have been falsely arrested and later convicted and put in prison. People are victims of ugly rumor or vicious slander.

My wife and I are friends with a Jewish woman who had an extremely painful childhood. She can still recall one Christmas when the other kids in the class, who hated the "Jew girl," as they put it, exchanged gifts. What she received for a gift was a bag of garbage.

I remember reading of a pastor who took a strong stand on a certain issue. Several members of his church board did not agree that he was doing the right thing. Instead of dealing with it intelligently and carefully and lovingly, they came at night and destroyed his children's little swing set in the backyard and slashed all four tires on his car.

My wife vividly recalls waiting in a medical office several years ago with one of our children. There she witnessed a young mother of three make one abusive statement after another to her children. The worst occurred when one child reached over to touch a picture, just to feel the frame, and the mother said, "If you touch that again, I'll break every finger on your hand."

You could think of a dozen other examples I'm sure. Certainly there are times when abuses and mistreatment must be reported to proper authorities, but more often than not the things we suffer are not criminal acts but rather unfair experiences that are hard to bear. And when those things happen, the greatest test of that experience is the test of attitude. If we're ripped off, we want to rip in return—only worse! It's our human nature. We want to get revenge; we want to get even. Just wait, we say. We'll get even. We'll get our own back. And so we wait for the perfect moment to pounce. And as we do, we feel the restricting confinement of that attitude. It binds us until we're held hostage by it, unable to be free, unable to live an enjoyable life.

Suddenly we come across a verse like 1 Peter 2:20 which says,

> For what credit is there if, when you sin and are harshly treated, you
> endure it with patience? But if when you do what is right and suffer
> for it you patiently endure it, this finds favor with God.

Yes, you read that correctly. (You may want to read it again, just to make sure.) When we read statements like that along with verses like Isaiah 55:8–9, we start to wonder how these things square with the truth that God is good. Remember those words from Isaiah's pen as he repeats God's message?

"For My thoughts are not your thoughts,
Neither are your ways My ways," declares the LORD.
"For as the heavens are higher than the earth,
So are My ways higher than your ways,
And My thoughts than your thoughts."

Look carefully at the contrasts. There is a vast difference between "My thoughts" and "your thoughts" says the Lord. "My ways" are not like "your ways." They are higher; they are far more profound, deep, mysterious—and I would even add, *surprising*.

Our human ways are based on what seems fair. We firmly believe that when someone does what is right, rewards and blessings result. When someone does what is wrong, there are serious consequences, even punishment. But that's our way, not necessarily God's way. At least not immediately. He's been known to allow unfair treatment to occur in the lives of some absolutely innocent folks—for reasons far more profound and deep than they or we could have imagined. How slowly He steps in!

JOSEPH'S MISTREATMENT

If anybody knew about unfair treatment, about mistreatment, about being an innocent victim on the receiving end, it was Joseph.

First, *he received unfair treatment from his family.* His brothers hated him, wanted to kill him, but sold him into slavery instead. Next, *his circumstances were unexpectedly restricted.* He became a slave in a land where he didn't even know the language. One minute he was a seventeen-year-old boy with his whole life before him, and the next he was totally at the mercy of—actually the property of—some stranger. Following all that, he was falsely accused. After earning the favor of his master,

Potiphar, the master's wife tried to seduce Joseph. As we saw in the previous chapter, when he didn't submit to her wishes, she lied and said, "This slave tried to rape me." As result of her lies, *he was unjustly put in prison and abandoned.*

JOSEPH'S IMPRISONMENT

That's where we find Joseph in this chapter. Having been unfairly treated, unexpectedly restricted by circumstances, and falsely accused, he is in prison. In fact, according to Genesis 40:15, he is in a *dungeon.* He's back in a pit again, this time at the very bottom of an Egyptian pit. He's starting all over again.

How old was Joseph? No one knows for sure. Probably in his late twenties. A bigger question is: Where was God? We can see God in the good things. We can even see Him in the questionable things. But where is God when all is unfair? Where is God when the dungeon experience occurs? Does His silence mean He's absent? We're not left to wonder.

Genesis 39:21 says, "The LORD was with Joseph." That's where God was. He was right there. He never left. He *never* left. He was *with* Joseph. Not only that, he did for Joseph what he had done before. He gave him favor in the eyes of others.

> But the LORD was with Joseph and extended kindness to him, and gave him favor in the sight of the chief jailer. And the chief jailer committed to Joseph's charge all the prisoners who were in the jail; so that whatever was done there, he was responsible for it. The chief jailer did not supervise anything under Joseph's charge because the LORD was with him; and whatever he did, the LORD made to prosper.
>
> Genesis 39:21–23

Twice we read in that short account, "The LORD was with Joseph," Joseph began to see the hand of God in his prison experience. In what could have been the direst of positions, the dreariest of places, Joseph prospered. Because of this, he was freed up to be used of God strategically in the lives of at least two men. Amazingly, he prospered in prison—of all places.

Aleksandr Solzhenitsyn painfully describes his spiritual awakening in some of the most powerful words of his entire book, *The Gulag Archipelago*. In his loneliness and pain, God came near.

> . . . In the intoxication of youthful successes I had felt myself to be infallible, and I was therefore cruel. In the surfeit of power I was a mur-derer, and an oppressor. In my most evil moments I was convinced that I was doing good, and I was well supplied with systematic arguments. And it was only when I lay there on rotting prison straw that I sensed within myself the first stirrings of good. Gradually, it was disclosed to me that the line separating good and evil passes not through states, not between classes, nor between political parties either—but right through every human heart—and through all human hearts. . . . So, bless you, prison, for having been in my life.[1]

The old Russian writer who spent eight years in the infamous Soviet Gulag camp system sounds like the psalmist, who wrote, "It is good for me that I was afflicted, that I may learn Thy statutes" (119:71).

Those dungeon experiences were good for me, because it was there that the Lord took away from me all the dreamy idealism of the spiritual life. Ultimately, Joseph was also able to say, "Bless you, prison, because it was *there* God became real."

False accusations put Joseph in prison, but it was the Lord who stayed near him and nurtured his soul while he was there. As a result, Joseph found favor even in the eyes of the chief jailer—what we might call the prison warden—to the point where the man trusted Joseph to supervise all the other prisoners. The warden trusted and respected Joseph so much that he "did not supervise anything under Joseph's charge because the LORD was with him; and whatever he did, the LORD made to prosper."

You see, the Lord God remained first in Joseph's life; He was the focus of his life. The lens of God's will stood between Joseph and his circumstances, enabling Joseph to see God in them, to read God in them—and enabling God to use him in them.

When a dungeon experience comes, the quickest and easiest response is to feel that you've been forgotten by God. I don't know if you read the cartoon "Ziggy," but I enjoy him—maybe because he often says the very things I've been thinking! One of my favorites shows Ziggy, with his big nose and bald head, standing on a mountain and staring far above him. The sky is dark and there is one lonely cloud up there. Ziggy yells, "Have I been put on hold for the rest of my life?"

You've felt like that, haven't you? "Lord, will You ever answer?" How often the heavens seem more like cold brass than God's loving abode. We cry out, but nothing comes in return.

Make no mistake about it, Joseph didn't deserve jail, but he responded to it beautifully. That's the marvel of the story. First and foremost in his life was his vital and consistent relationship with his Lord. And because of that, God used him in strategic and significant ways.

JOSEPH'S CELLMATES

> Then it came about after these things the cupbearer and the baker for the king of Egypt offended their lord, the king of Egypt. And Pharaoh was furious with his two officials, the chief cupbearer and the chief baker. So he put them in confinement in the house of the captain of the bodyguard, in the jail, the same place where Joseph was imprisoned.
>
> Genesis 40:1–3

A cupbearer was the person who tasted the wine and food of the king before he ate or drank. That way, if it was poisoned, "So long, cupbearer," but "Long live Pharaoh"! He also would not allow poorly prepared food to be served to the pharaoh since he was responsible for watching the monarch's diet. This led to a very close relationship, a relationship of trust between the two men. Often the king of the land would confide in the cupbearer. If you recall, Nehemiah was the cupbearer to the king of his day and had a close, personal relationship with him. In many ways the cupbearer was the most trusted man of the court. If that trust was ever broken, serious consequences followed.

Something like that must have happened, because the cupbearer to Pharaoh landed in jail—as had also the king's baker. (He was another person on whom the pharaoh relied, because whatever he prepared passed into the mouth of the Egyptian ruler). The specifics of what had happened to bring about this falling out and punishment, we're never told. All we know is that they "offended their lord" and he was "furious with his two officials." Maybe the biscuits fell that morning, and later there were too many jalapeños in the chili, and the cupbearer didn't warn Pharaoh! It must have been related to the food because their jobs were interrelated. But whatever it was, it made Pharaoh so angry that he said, "Get out of my sight!" and had them both thrown in jail. And since God's ways are deep and profound, it happened to be the same jail where Joseph was imprisoned.

Isn't it remarkable how often God brings alongside us people who are going through, or have gone through, similar experiences? Isn't it amazing, when we are hurting, God brings alongside us others who understand our pain? That is certainly true here. Joseph and these two men may have ended up in prison for different reasons, but they found themselves in the same place, sharing similar miseries. And out of his own experience, Joseph was able to minister to them.

Remember, though, this was possible only because the Lord was first and foremost in Joseph's life. Because he was free of bitterness, he became a useful instrument in the mighty hand of God. If any resentment, hostility, or desire for vengeance remained, we read nothing of it in this narrative. I'm convinced it was not there.

The plot thickens:

> And the captain of the bodyguard put Joseph in charge of them, and he took care of them; and they were in confinement for some time. Then the cupbearer and the baker for the king of Egypt, who were confined in jail, they both had a dream the same night, each man with his own dream and each dream with its own interpretation. When Joseph came to them in the morning and observed them, behold, they were dejected. And he asked Pharaoh's officials who

were with him in confinement in his master's house, "Why are your faces so sad today?"

Genesis 40:4–7

I smile as I read this, because if anybody ought to have had a sad face, it should have been Joseph. His plight was much worse than theirs. They were there on a whim of the Pharaoh and surely would not be there forever. But Joseph had been accused by the chief executioner's wife and didn't know if he'd ever see the light of day. But in spite of his own circumstance, he noticed the plight of these two men.

When your heart is right, even though the bottom may have dropped out of your life, it is remarkable how sensitive you can be to somebody else in need. They don't even have to spell it out. Rather than saying, "You think you've got a lot to complain about, listen to my tale of woe!" Joseph said, "How come you're so sad today, guys? What's wrong?" I admit it may be stating the obvious to ask this in a dungeon, but it shows Joseph's ability to think beyond his own immediate cares and needs in order to minister mercy to others.

One of the beautiful things about the right attitude is that, with it, every day has sunshine. You don't have to have cloudless days for there to be sunshine days.

I've often enjoyed repeating the true story of an incident in the life of Thomas Edison that illustrates perfectly the benefits of a positive attitude. Edison's son, Charles, writes of the event about his father in his book titled, *The Electric Thomas Edison.*

[One] December evening the cry of "Fire!" echoed through the plant. Spontaneous combustion had broken out in the film room. Within moments all the packing compounds, celluloid for records, film and other flammable goods had gone up with a whoosh. . . .

When I couldn't find Father, I became concerned. Was he safe? With all his assets going up in smoke, would his spirit be broken? He was 67, no age to begin anew. Then I saw him in the plant yard, running toward me.

"Where's Mom?" he shouted. "Go get her! Tell her to get her friends! They'll never see a fire like this again!"[2]

Can you believe it? Rather than saying, "Oh, God, what did I do to deserve this? Sixty-seven years I've faithfully lived my life, and this is what I get in return," he says, "Hey, son, get your mother. This is one unbelievable sight! Look at that fire!"

Edison's son continues,

> At 5:30 the next morning, when the fire was barely under control, he called his employees together and announced, "We're rebuilding!"
>
> One man was told to lease all the machine shops in the area. Another, to obtain a wrecking crane from the Erie Railroad Company. Then, almost as an afterthought he added, "Oh, by the way. Anybody know where we can get some money?"
>
> Later on he explained, "You can always make capital out of disaster. We've just cleared out a bunch of old rubbish! We'll build bigger and better on these ruins." With that he rolled up his coat for a pillow, curled up on a table and immediately fell asleep.[3]

Joseph did a similar thing. He said, "How come you guys have such sad faces? What's going on in this dungeon?"

> Then they said to him, "We have had a dream and there is no one to interpret it."
>
> Genesis 40:8a

I bet Joseph had to bite his lip when he heard that! They were worried about a dream they'd each had and could not interpret. Little did they know that they had the dreamer of all dreamers sitting in their midst.

> Then Joseph said to them, "Do not interpretations belong to God? Tell it to me, please."
>
> Genesis 40:8b

Actually, it's rather amazing that Joseph would want to have anything to do with dreams. The last time he did that, remember what happened? He told his brothers about his dreams and it was "Operation Pit City." He wound up in an Egyptian slave market. You'd think he would say, "Not me, man! I'm off of dreams forever." But not Joseph. He said, "Oh, really? A dream, huh? Tell me about it."

That's what a positive attitude will do. It gets you beyond common hurdles. It will clear the deck. It will free you from hang-ups. It will show you an opportunity for ministry you never would have touched with a ten-foot pole.

So Joseph said, "Only God can interpret dreams, but tell me about yours."

The First Dream Interpreted

> So the chief cupbearer told his dream to Joseph, and said to him, "In my dream, behold, there was a vine in front of me; and on the vine were three branches. And as it was budding, its blossoms came out, and its clusters produced ripe grapes. Now Pharaoh's cup was in my hand; so I took the grapes and squeezed them into Pharaoh's cup, and I put the cup into Pharaoh's hand."
>
> Genesis 40:9–11

The cupbearer said, "There was this vine that grew up, and it had three branches. It budded and blossomed and the clusters produced ripe grapes. I took the grapes and squeezed them into Pharaoh's cup, and put the cup in his hand. What in the world does all that mean?"

> Then Joseph said to him, "This is the interpretation of it: the three branches are three days; within three more days Pharaoh will lift up your head and restore you to your office; and you will put Pharaoh's cup into his hand according to your former custom when you were his cupbearer. Only keep me in mind when it goes well with you, and please do me a kindness by mentioning me to Pharaoh, and get me out of this house. For I was in fact kidnapped from the land of the Hebrews, and even here I have done nothing that they should have put me into the dungeon."
>
> Genesis 40:12–15

"Here's what this means," said Joseph. "The three branches are three days. In three days you will be restored to your former office as cupbearer." Then he added, "When that happens, remember me," and he explained a bit about his own plight and his innocence.

Here was Joseph's humanity emerging. I love this, because it shows us that Joseph was a real person, not some plaster saint. He knew that sometimes an inmate got out of prison by knowing the right person. And nobody was closer to Pharaoh than the chief cupbearer. Hopefully, when the cupbearer returned to Pharaoh's presence and had his ear again, he would say, "Master, there's a man you should look kindly toward."

"Keep me in mind when it goes well with you," said Joseph. "Remember me." Can't blame him for that.

In the meantime, however, the baker had been listening in on the conversation, and he must have thought, *Maybe my dream is good news too.* So he said to Joseph, "How about my dream?"

The Second Dream Interpreted

> When the chief baker saw that he had interpreted favorably, he said to Joseph, "I also saw in my dream, and behold, there were three baskets of white bread on my head; and in the top basket there were some of all sorts of baked food for Pharaoh, and the birds were eating them out of the basket on my head."
>
> Genesis 40:16–17

"What does that mean?" asked the baker. Joseph said, "Well, this is a little different."

You have to respect Joseph's integrity. He knew the dream meant that the guy was going to be killed. Who wants to deliver that message? He could have told the baker anything, made up a lie, and he would have never known the difference. Or, by the time he did, it wouldn't have mattered anyway. But Joseph was a man who told the truth. He was not winning friends; he was representing God.

> Then Joseph answered and said, "This is its interpretation: the three baskets are three days; within three more days Pharaoh will lift up

your head from you and will hang you on a tree; and the birds will
eat your flesh off you."

Genesis 40:18–19

"The three baskets are three days," said Joseph. "This means that in three days you will be executed." The news was grim, but Joseph told him the truth.

I emphasize this point because I want you to understand that having a contagious, positive attitude toward God does not mean living unrealistically where you tell everybody nice, upbeat things all the time, whether they are true or not. I believe in thinking positively, but I don't believe in phony baloney. I believe in thinking positively, because I believe that's the only way Christians really think aright, as we see things through Christ's eyes. But that's not the same as thinking unrealistically or living in a dream world or saying something to someone just to make them feel good.

Joseph said, in effect, "My friend, your days are numbered." And that is exactly what happened. The events involving both men came about precisely as Joseph had predicted.

> Thus it came about on the third day, which was Pharaoh's birthday,
> that he made a feast for all his servants; and he lifted up the head of
> the chief cupbearer and the head of the chief baker among his servants.
> And he restored the chief cupbearer to his office, and he put the cup
> into Pharaoh's hand; but he hanged the chief baker, just as Joseph had
> interpreted to them.

Genesis 40:20–22

JOSEPH'S DISAPPOINTMENT

When Joseph saw the cupbearer taken from the prison, he must have thought, *Now's my chance! This guy has Pharaoh's ear. He'll get me out of here.* We don't know whether Joseph knew what happened to these men, but when their release came within the predicted time, he must have figured that, with God's help, he had given the correct interpretation of the dreams. So he waited hopefully for his opportunity to be released and set free. Surely, he anticipated the warden coming in and announcing, "You've been set free, Joseph. You've been remembered and vindicated."

Though he had done no wrong, though he had told only the truth, though he had specifically requested to be remembered—only silence prevailed. Joseph's long-awaited hopes were dashed.

> Yet the chief cupbearer did not remember Joseph, but forgot him.
>
> Genesis 40:23

> Now it happened at the end of two full years that Pharaoh had a dream. . . .
>
> Genesis 41:1

Talk about *disappointment!* Instead of being remembered and rewarded, he was forgotten for two more years. It's easy to overlook that little fact buried in the midst of all these dream sequences and their interpretations. But for two years after the cupbearer left, Joseph remained buried in that dungeon. Notice the emphasis: two *full* years. Two long, monotonous, miserable years!

What did Joseph think about during that time? The human tendency would be: "Will I be on hold forever, Lord? I never deserved to be here to begin with, but I didn't complain or try to escape. I also interpreted the dreams correctly and walked close to You month after month. I did what You wanted me to do. I've served You faithfully. What I said was true! And the man forgot me." In fact, it seems like *You have forgotten me!* No, there was none of that. This remarkable man, victimized again and again, continued to wait—to trust—to hope—to lean on God.

JOSEPH'S SITUATION THEN—AND OURS TODAY

The story of Joseph's mistreatment, disappointment, and abandonment resonates with all of us. Wives without husbands, husbands without wives, children without parents, parents without children, men and women without jobs, pastors no longer in ministry, former pastors' wives no longer in demand or, for that matter, respected. Prisoners locked away, haunted by their crimes they committed (or did not commit!), plagued by loneliness and abandonment. This story has relevance woven all the way through it.

Unfair treatment, mistreatment, comes in many forms, but most of it falls into one of four categories. First is *undeserved treatment from family*. It's possible for children to mistreat parents just as readily as parents can mistreat children—even grown children.

At the seminary where I serve we train some of the finest men and women you could ever hope to meet. They are intellectually gifted, spiritually in tune, and devoted to doing the Lord's work wherever He may call them to serve. On the surface, they seem to "have it all together." But the closer we grow together and the longer we spend time with one another, the more I realize how many come from homes that were anything but wholesome and affirming.

I interview most of our graduates several weeks before they receive their degrees. It is amazing what you uncover from others' lives once you're behind closed doors. There are often tears of heartache as they tell of strained relationships with one or both parents. Thankfully, there are wonderful exceptions, but it isn't uncommon to hear our grads tell sad stories of broken and abusive homes, angry mothers and absent dads. Every year there are those who receive their hard-earned master's degree without one person from their family present to applaud their achievement.

One young man told me his dad hadn't spoken to him for four years— ever since the son chose not to pursue a law degree as his father (an attorney) had hoped, but rather to study theology and serve Christ's church. As I shook his hand and presented him with his master of theology diploma, our eyes met—and we then embraced as he wept. At that epochal moment in his life, he felt, again, the sting of abandonment.

Abusive mistreatment within the family takes many forms and leaves many scars.

The second category of mistreatment is the *unexpected restriction of circumstances*. This happens when you are suddenly confined, either emotionally or physically. You either can't get beyond your own emotions or your physical circumstances. Sudden injury or a traumatic disease can leave a person disabled, feeling terribly alone. The scars from an abusive past can result in long, dungeonlike years of pain as the person struggles to recover. A close, personal friend of mine is going through the horror of helping his wife recover from a childhood of sexual abuse. I haven't the space, nor would it be appropriate, to describe the difficulty of that journey. Among many other by-products of that lengthy recovery is the loss of their own marital intimacy . . . for more than two years. He longs to hold his wife and enjoy the delights of romance and intimate pleasures, but that is not to be. Not now. Maybe never.

These unexpected restrictions keep people from flying free, from soaring, from enjoying life.

The third kind of mistreatment is *untrue accusations*. You don't have to live very long on this earth before people begin to say false things about you. It even happens to young children. The tragedy is that those false words are heard by people who don't know any better and they believe them. These untrue statements become as impossible to correct as catching feathers from a torn pillow on a windy day. Before long, you throw up your arms in apprehension and frustration, saying, "How can I ever set the record straight?"

Sometime ago, the rumor was going around in the Northwest that I'd been married before. If they knew how young Cynthia and I were when we married the first and only time back in 1955, they would never make a statement like that! It was untrue, yet the word began to spread, and many believed it and told others of it. What could we do to correct the record? Others, of course, have had much more scandalous, much more painful untrue accusations made about them.

The fourth category of mistreatment is *unfair abandonment*. In some ways, this may be the most painful of all. It hurts.

Many women can identify with this. You helped your husband through school. You saw the vision and the future of his life as well as the potential of his gifts, and you, the faithful wife, worked hard. He got the glory, he got the degrees, he got the job, he got the name, he got the credit—and then he left. Today, you don't even know where he is. You helped him. You committed yourself to that marriage. You may have even given birth to his children. You stood with him when there was very little in return, and he has abandoned you. He took the money and ran.

Some of you have graciously loaned a lot of money to someone and that person has exploited your generosity. He or she is not paying anything back. You're out maybe thousands of dollars. You have been unfairly abandoned.

Some of you have worked with another person to build a business. You labored willingly behind the scenes. He got the credit, and you did most of the work—plodding along year after year after year. Then, finally, when it all began to pay off, he dropped you like a bad habit.

Some of you have been misjudged and abandoned by friends because of it. Perhaps even by your brothers and sisters in the local church, because false statements were made against you which they believed. That's painful.

But I want to tell you something: That may be difficult for you to accept, but you need to understand that it is in that kind of pain that God gives His best messages. It's what C. S. Lewis calls "God's megaphone." In *The Problem of Pain*, he writes: "God whispers to us in our pleasures, speaks in our conscience, but shouts in our pains."[4]

We have two choices: We can become disillusioned and embittered, or we can use that difficulty as a platform for putting our hope and trust in the living God.

Disillusionment is a dangerous, slippery slope. First we become disillusioned about our fellow man. Then we move on to cynicism. Before long, we trust no one, not even God. We've been burned. We've been taken advantage of; we've been mistreated. I have never met an individual who was truly disillusioned with mankind who has not also become disillusioned with God. The two go together. Cynicism is spawned in such a context.

The cause of disillusionment and the cure for it can be expressed in almost the same simple words. The *cause* of disillusionment is *putting one's complete hope and trust in people.* Putting people on a pedestal, focusing on them, finding our security in them. Being so horizontally locked in that the person takes the place of God, even *becomes* God. Your complete hope can rest in one person. It can be your child. It can be your parent. It can be a business partner, a friend, a pastor, a coach, a mate. And when the feet of clay crumble (as surely they will), total disillusionment sets in.

What's the cure? *Putting our complete hope and trust in the living Lord.* When we do that, the simplest messages from God calm our spirits.

Christian Reger is a man who did exactly that. Christian Reger spent four years in the infamous Dachau, imprisoned by the Nazis from 1941 to 1945. His crime? He was a member of the Confessing Church, one of the German state churches that took a stand against the Nazis in the 1930s and 1940s. Martin Niemoeller and Dietrich Bonhoeffer both ministered in that church. As a whole, it was a church that stood for the truth, but Christian Reger was turned over to the Nazis by the organist of his local church. He was shipped hundreds of miles away to spend the next four years in the concentration camp of Dachau, outside Munich.

Philip Yancey tells this man's memorable story in his book *Where Is God When It Hurts?*

> Christian Reger will tell the horror stories if you ask. But he will never stop there. He goes on to share his faith—how at Dachau, he was visited by a God who loves.
>
> "Nietzsche said a man can undergo torture if he knows the why of his life," Reger told me. "But I, here at Dachau, learned something far greater. I learned to know the Who of my life. He was enough to sustain me then, and is enough to sustain me still."[5]

A CLOSING PLEA

Listen to me, victims of mistreatment; more importantly, please listen to God's truth. He has a hundred different messages to give you during a hundred different dungeon experiences. He knows just the right message at just the right time, and all it takes to receive it is a sensitive, obedient, trusting heart. Not one preoccupied with revenge or bitterness or hostility, but a heart that says, "Lord, God, help me now. Right at this moment.

Deliver me from my own prison. Help me to see beyond the darkness, to see Your hand. As I am being crushed, remold me. Help me to see You in this abandonment, this rejection." Pray that prayer. Turn your trial into trust as you look to God to tenderly use that affliction, that dungeon, that abandonment for His purpose. I plead with you—do that today! If Joseph could survive those years of mistreatment, loneliness, and loss, I am confident you can too!

I know your world is not filled with Egyptian dungeons or dreams that need to be interpreted, or even Nazi war camps. Your mistreatment comes in a completely different package. But whatever form it takes, it hurts. You feel the horrible rejection. You've done what is right but you've been treated wrongly.

In the midst of all this, remember, God has not abandoned you. He has not forgotten you. He never left. He understands the heartache brought on by the evil which He mysteriously permits so that He might bring you to a tender, sensitive walk with Him. God is good, Jesus Christ is real —your present circumstances notwithstanding. My prayer is that He will do for you what He did for Joseph.

May He give you the grace to endure.

CHAPTER FOUR

Remembered and Promoted

P ain, when properly handled, can shape a life for greatness. History is replete with stories of those whose struggles and scars formed the foundation for remarkable achievements. In fact, it was because of their hardship they gained what they needed to achieve greatness.

A young woman sang a solo in front of a large audience. Her vocal technique was splendid, her intonation excellent, her range significant. Coincidentally, the man who had written the piece of music she sang was sitting in the audience. When the young woman finished, the person sitting beside the composer leaned over and said, "Well, what do you think of her?" Softly the composer responded, "She will be really great when something happens to break her heart."

For a long time in my life, I wrestled with that concept. It seemed to be a cruel philosophy. Why should anyone need to suffer? What do you mean, "There are benefits that come only through struggles?" I have now come full circle. I agree with A. W. Tozer, who said: "It is doubtful whether God can bless a man greatly until He has hurt him deeply."[1] I could mention numerous examples, but certainly no life evidences this truth more clearly than the life of Joseph.

For the most part, Joseph's experiences thus far have been somber. He may have been born a favored son, but his life was filled with disappointment, mistreatment, and rejection, with fear and false accusations, with slavery and abandonment. We left Joseph alone in prison as we ended the previous chapter. Now, after a gap of two full years, we pick up his story again.

Remember, when we left him, he had told the cupbearer two years earlier, "Now that I've told you the meaning of your dream, don't forget me. Keep me in mind when things go well with you, and when you get promoted. Please do me the kindness of mentioning me to Pharaoh, and get me out of this place. Remember me." But the cupbearer failed to remember or mention Joseph. Only three days after Joseph said this, the man was released and restored to his former position as chief cupbearer to Pharaoh. He promptly forgot all about his days in the dungeon, as well as his cell mate, Joseph.

Two full years passed after that event—a long time to be forgotten. We may find ourselves asking, "After all Joseph had been through, why would something like this happen?" He had been obedient to God and was earlier promoted because "God was with him." The answer is that God was still at work in his life. Another Bible character who learned through hardship was Job.

PROMISES OF DIVINE PROMOTION

Dear old Job, beaten black and blue by calamity, the death of ten children (imagine it!), the destruction of his home, the loss of everything he owned, including his own health. He didn't even have the comfort of caring friends. He had nothing. I don't think anyone would cluck his tongue at Job for saying what he does in meditating on his plight, searching for God's answers.

> "Oh that I knew where I might find Him,
> That I might come to His seat!

I would present my case before Him
And fill my mouth with arguments.

I would learn the words which He would answer,
And perceive what He would say to me.

Would He contend with me by the greatness of His power?
No, surely He would pay attention to me.

There the upright would reason with Him;
And I would be delivered forever from my Judge.

Behold, I go forward but He is not there,
And backward, but I cannot perceive Him;

When He acts on the left, I cannot behold Him;
He turns on the right, I cannot see Him."

Job 23:3–9

Job is saying, "I wish I could find God. I wish He and I could just sit down and talk openly about my situation, and I could ask Him why I'm going through these things. I want to have all my 'Why?' questions answered. I want to have all my 'How long?' problems solved."

Despite everything he has been through, Job still believes that God will listen to him. "Would He slap me across the face and say, 'Be quiet, Job, and sit there'? No, He would pay attention to me."

Though he believes this, Job still questions why: "What He's doing, I don't know. Where He is, I can't find Him. What He sees, I can't see. *But* I know this . . . I *know* this," says Job. I love this statement of faith:

"But He knows the way I take;
When He has tried me, I shall come forth as gold.

My foot has held fast to His path;
I have kept His way and not turned aside.

"I have not departed from the command of His lips;
I have treasured the words of His mouth more than
my necessary food."

Job 23:10–12

The key phrase in that statement is at the beginning of it: "when He has tried me." You see, there is no hurry-up process for finding and shaping gold. The process of discovering, processing, purifying, and shaping gold is a lengthy, painstaking process. Affliction is gold in the making for the child of God, and God is the one who determines how long the process takes. He alone is the Refiner.

Job was not saying, "When He has tried me, I will make a million!" Or, "When He has tried me, I'll get everything back that I lost." Or, "When He has tried me, my wife will say she's sorry and will make things right." Or, "When He has tried me, everything will be like it once was." No, it's not the externals that are promised, it's the internals. The Lord promised Job, "When the process is finished, you'll come forth as *gold*. Then, you'll be ready to serve me where I choose. Then, you'll be able to handle whatever promotion comes your way."

This was where Joseph was when we left him. He was still in process. His gold was still being refined. His heart was still being broken by affliction and abandonment.

THE TEST: DARKNESS BEFORE THE DAWN

Those *two full years* for Joseph were neither exciting nor eventful. They represented a long, dull, monotonous, unspectacular, slow-moving grind. Month after month after month of . . . well, *nothing*. Not even the Genesis account attempts to make those years seem meaningful. Because they weren't.

That's what it's like when you're in a period of waiting. Nothing's happening! Wait. Wait. Wait. Wait.

On the other hand, it only *seems* like nothing is happening. In reality, a whole lot is happening. Events are occurring apart from our involvement.

Furthermore, *we* are being strengthened. We are being established. We are being perfected. We are being refined. Refined into pure gold.

We're back to my earlier comment—he's being shaped for greatness. All whom God uses greatly are first hidden in the secret of His presence, away from the pride of man. It is there our vision clears. It is there the silt drops from the current of our life and our faith begins to grasp His arm. Abraham waited for the birth of Isaac. Moses didn't lead the Exodus until he was eighty. Elijah waited beside the brook. Noah waited 120 years for rain. Paul was hidden away for three years in Arabia. The list doesn't end. God is working while His people are waiting, waiting, waiting. Joseph is being shaped for a significant future.

That's what's happening. For the present time, nothing. For the future, everything!

THE TURNING POINT: PHARAOH'S DREAM

After those two full years, Joseph experienced a turning point in his life—on a day that seemed like any other day. That morning dawned like every other morning over the previous two years. Just like the morning that dawned before Moses saw the burning bush. Just like the morning that dawned before David was anointed by Samuel as the king-elect. For Joseph, just another dungeon day—except for one little matter Joseph knew nothing about: The night before Pharaoh had a bad dream.

THE DREAM DECLARED

Now it happened at the end of two full years that Pharaoh had a dream, and behold, he was standing by the Nile. And lo, from the Nile there came up seven cows, sleek and fat; and they grazed in the marsh grass. Then behold, seven other cows came up after them from the Nile, ugly and gaunt, and they stood by the other cows on the bank of the Nile. And the ugly and gaunt cows ate up the seven sleek and fat cows. Then Pharaoh awoke. And he fell asleep and dreamed a second time; and behold, seven ears of grain came up on a single stalk, plump and good. Then behold, seven ears, thin and scorched by the east wind, sprouted up after them. And the thin ears swallowed up the seven plump and full ears. Then Pharaoh awoke, and behold, it was a dream.

Genesis 41:1–7

The king of the land had a dream, and in it he saw seven fat, sleek cattle coming up out of the marshy Nile delta. Then seven ugly, gaunt, starving cows came up from the same river and devoured the fat, sleek cows.

Pharaoh awoke, perhaps thinking that huge meal he'd eaten before he went to bed wasn't setting too well on his stomach. Before long he fell back to sleep, and his dream continued. This time he saw a stalk of grain with seven plump and healthy ears. But then seven lean ears, scorched from the east wind, sprang up and devoured the seven healthy ears of grain.

When Pharaoh awoke, he remembered what he had dreamed, and he was disturbed by it.

Now it came about in the morning that his spirit was troubled, so he sent and called for all the magicians of Egypt, and all its wise men. And Pharaoh told them his dreams, but there was no one who could interpret them to Pharaoh.

Genesis 41:8

There's an interesting point about the term rendered "magicians" here. When that word was originally translated from the ancient Hebrew Scriptures into Greek, the translators used a term that meant "men versed in the sacred writings."

Why mention this? Because it tells us that all these men were very intelligent. They were considered the wisest men in the land. They spent their time deciphering everything from the Egyptian hieroglyphic texts to studying the movement of the stars in the heavens. But as wise as they were, they could not tell Pharaoh what his dream meant. Actually, I admire their honesty. They could have made something up, but they didn't. They said, "We don't know what your dream means."

All of a sudden, the light dawned on Pharaoh's chief cupbearer.

> Then the chief cupbearer spoke to Pharaoh, saying, "I would make mention today of my own offenses. Pharaoh was furious with his servants, and he put me in confinement in the house of the captain of the bodyguard, both me and the chief baker. And we had a dream on the same night, he and I; each of us dreamed according to the interpretation of his own dream. Now a Hebrew youth was with us there, a servant of the captain of the bodyguard, and we related them to him, and he interpreted our dreams for us. To each one he interpreted according to his own dream. And it came about that just as he interpreted for us, so it happened; he restored me in my office, but he hanged him."
>
> Then Pharaoh sent and called for Joseph, and they hurriedly brought him out of the dungeon; and when he had shaved himself and changed his clothes, he came to Pharaoh.
>
> Genesis 41:9–14

When Pharaoh heard that there was someone around who could tell him what this troubling dream meant, he naturally said, "Go get the man."

Now remember, Joseph knew nothing of what had been taking place in Pharaoh's palace. He had no idea what was coming. He was back there in the dungeon, when suddenly the chains clanked and the bars moved and the ropes lifted and he found himself being pulled up out of the pit.

There's an interesting sidelight I want you to note here. When Pharaoh sent for Joseph, the guards quickly got him out of the dungeon. But instead of rushing into Pharaoh's presence, Joseph "shaved himself and changed his clothes" before he went to Pharaoh.

Joseph prepared himself to meet the king!

After all that time in prison, Joseph was disheveled and tattered and no doubt heavily bearded. Normally, the Egyptians were clean-shaven. He must have thought, *If I'm going to appear before the king, I've got to do something about the way I look. My appearance must be appropriate if I am to enter his presence.* So he shaved and washed and changed his clothes.

The Dream Interpreted

Pause and imagine this long-awaited moment. It had been years since Joseph had been a part of the real world. Consider the startling contrast—from a dingy dungeon to Pharaoh's palace. What a rush! There he stood, freshly shaven and wearing a clean robe—and the Lord was still with him, as we can see in his first response to Pharaoh.

> And Pharaoh said to Joseph, "I have had a dream, but no one can interpret it; and I have heard it said about you, that when you hear a dream you can interpret it." Joseph then answered Pharaoh, saying, "It is not in me; God will give Pharaoh a favorable answer."
>
> Genesis 41:15–16

"According to my sources," said Pharaoh, "you're the guy with the answers. Tell me what my dream means, and I'll make it worth your while."

"Wait a minute," said Joseph. "I don't have the answers, but God does."

The New International Version translates this, "I cannot do it, but God will give Pharaoh the answer he desires."

Talk about humility. Talk about absolute integrity. This was Joseph's moment in court, his golden opportunity to say, "Do you realize that I could have been out of that place two years ago if that dummy standing right over there hadn't forgotten me? Do you realize I could have been handling dreams for you for these past two years? I could have saved you a lot of lost sleep. So if you expect me to help you now, how about getting rid of him and making things right with me?" But there was none of that.

Instead, Joseph said, "No, I'm not the one with the answers. But I serve a God who is. And we'll both listen to Him, and He'll tell us what He wants us to learn."

He said, in effect, "Pharaoh, there's a God up there behind those stars that your soothsayers are always gazing at but have no relationship with. And I'm here to tell you, He and He alone is the One who handles dreams." When that happens, he says, literally, "God will give Pharaoh peace." Isn't that great? "Pharaoh, God will bring shalom to you. He will give a peaceful answer. And if it's from God, it'll be right."

You know why Joseph could be so humble and speak so openly? Because his heart had been broken. Because he had been tried by the fire of affliction. Because while his external circumstances seemed almost unbearable during those years, his internal condition had been turned into pure gold. We are now witnessing the benefits of enduring affliction with one's eyes on God.

Throughout the rest of Joseph's life, from age 30 to age 110 when he died, we will hear not one word of resentment on his heart or from his lips. Not a word of blame against the brothers who sold him into slavery, not a word of bitterness against Potiphar's wife, not a word of rebuke against the cupbearer who had forgotten him. Joseph was eventually in a position to get even with all of them. But he didn't. More on that later. Let's return to this scene.

Pharaoh told Joseph all about his dream, about the different cows and the contrasting ears of grain. He then waited for the answer. Calmly and methodically, Joseph interpreted the dream.

> Now Joseph said to Pharaoh, "Pharaoh's dreams are one and the same; God has told to Pharaoh what He is about to do. The seven good cows are seven years; and the seven good ears are seven years; the dreams are one and the same. And the seven lean and ugly cows that came up after them are seven years, and the seven thin ears scorched by the east wind shall be seven years of famine. It is as I have spoken to Pharaoh: God has shown to Pharaoh what He is about to do. Behold, seven years of great abundance are coming in all the land of Egypt; and after them seven years of famine will come, and all the abundance will be forgotten in the land of Egypt; and the famine will ravage the land. So the abundance will be unknown in the land because of that subsequent famine; for it will be very severe. Now as for the repeating of the dream to Pharaoh twice, it means that the matter is determined by God, and God will quickly bring it about.
>
> Genesis 41:25–32

After Joseph heard about the dream, he said, "Through me, God is going to tell you what He is about to do. I'm just the messenger." Then he proceeds to interpret the dream for Pharaoh. "Both dreams mean the same thing: Egypt is going to have seven years of abundance—bumper crops everywhere. After that will come seven years of famine, which will be so intense that people will forget there ever were days of plenty. Not only will God's plan be carried out, but you can count on this: God's timing will be exact."

God! God! God! God! God! All the way through the answer, Joseph refers to God. Instead of calling attention to himself, he points Pharaoh to Jehovah. It isn't *I*, it's the Lord God! Here was a man who had truly humbled himself under the mighty hand of God.

Joseph then added a few words of counsel:

> "And now let Pharaoh look for a man discerning and wise, and set
> him over the land of Egypt."
>
> Genesis 41:33

Along with this recommendation, he also gave some very specific words of advice for procedures Pharaoh should follow. Egypt was going to need a strict, well-organized rationing process. When you have plenty, you eat plenty. You spend plenty. You don't save.

So Joseph said, "You need to have a man who can take responsibility for managing those seven years of fruitfulness, a man who will oversee the building of granaries and make certain that a portion of the grain is put into storage. When the famine strikes and wipes out this fertile land, you and your people will be able to live off those rations. Therefore, you need a man of discipline and foresight who can be trusted to handle the job. You need a good manager." But never once did he say, "I'd like the job. I've interpreted your dreams; I deserve the position."

THE REWARD: JOSEPH'S PROMOTION

> Now the proposal seemed good to Pharaoh and to all his servants.
> Then Pharaoh said to his servants, "Can we find a man like this, in
> whom is a divine spirit?"
>
> Genesis 41:37–38

There stood Joseph right before him, meeting all the requirements. But even then, when it seemed appropriate for Joseph to volunteer; he restrained. The king, however, knew Joseph was the man for the job.

Humility When Promoted

> So Pharaoh said to Joseph, "Since God has informed you of all this, there is no one so discerning and wise as you are. You shall be over my house, and according to your command all my people shall do homage; only in the throne I will be greater than you."
>
> Genesis 41:39–40

Who isn't impressed with Joseph's self-control? Refusing to manipulate the moment or drop hints, he simply stood there and waited. Somehow in the loneliness of his recent years, abandoned and forgotten in prison, he had learned to let the Lord have His way, in His time, for His purposes! Absent of selfish ambition, Joseph refused to promote himself. How refreshing—how rare!

How many of us have maneuvered or plotted to get our own way, only to live to regret it? One of the most embarrassing memories many people have is the day they got what they schemed and manipulated to acquire—only to see it dissolve right in their hands. That was not the kind of promotion Joseph wanted.

If God was in it, God would do it. That's precisely what happened here. God was in it and God did it. Pharaoh said to Joseph, "Since God told you all this, there is obviously no one as discerning or as wise as you. Therefore, I'm putting you in command of everything. The only person you answer to—the only person with more authority—is me. You're second in command. You're now my prime minister." Do you know what Pharaoh saw in Joseph? Gold.

The word *discernment* suggests the ability to have shrewd insight into a situation and act constructively in times of need. Joseph was a man who could do this and much, much more. He understood how to assess a situation and make the right moves, even under pressure. He understood this, because it was through pressure that he had been refined into gold.

Exalted over All Egypt

> And Pharaoh said to Joseph, "See I have set you over all the land of Egypt." Then Pharaoh took off his signet ring from his hand, and put it on Joseph's hand, and clothed him in garments of fine linen, and put the gold necklace around his neck. And he had him ride in his second chariot; and they proclaimed before him, "Bow the knee!" And he set him over all the land of Egypt.
>
> Genesis 41:41–43

Pharaoh swept his hand out wide, so as to include all that vast land of Egypt, and said, "It's all yours, Joseph." Then he took off his signet ring and put it on Joseph's hand.

You know what that ring signified, don't you? It was the platinum charge card of that day. It was the way the king stamped the invoices, the laws, or anything else he wanted to verify or validate with his seal. Now Joseph had that ring on his finger, placed there by the Pharaoh himself. Joseph wore the authority of the king's imprint.

Along with this, Pharaoh gave him fine garments made of linen and, appropriately, placed a gold necklace around his neck. He was even given a royal chariot.

Only a few hours before, Joseph was a scruffy, ragged, and forgotten prisoner in the dungeon. Now he was royally garbed, wore a gold necklace around his neck, had Pharaoh's ring on his finger, and riding in a fabulous chariot. And the people everywhere were commanded to "Bow the knee!"

Joseph's Cinderella-like promotion was incredible. But when God determines the time is right, that's the way He operates.

> Now Joseph was thirty years old when he stood before Pharaoh, king of Egypt. And Joseph went out from the presence of Pharaoh, and went through all the land of Egypt.
>
> Genesis 41:46

This is an excellent opportunity to shift the scene for a moment and look at all this from the perspective of the guy who's out working in the fields, moving stones for one of those interminable, ever-ongoing pyramid projects. He knows nothing at all about what's just happened in the dungeon and throne room. All he knows is that some young upstart, some foreigner, has maneuvered his way into Pharaoh's good graces. And he is being told, "Bow your knee to this man!"

"Oh, man, look at that!" says the workman. "Who does he think he is? Who did he bribe to get all this? He must know somebody. That's the way it is up there in the court."

Given that same situation, we'd probably think the same thing. Back in the Vietnam era we often heard the phrase "Never trust anyone over thirty." Today, given the large segment of aging populace, we are more likely to hear, "Never trust anyone *under* thirty."

Job himself said, "It is not only the old who are wise, not only the aged who understand what is right" (Job 32:9, NIV). Gray hair is no guarantee of wisdom, nor is youth necessarily a sign of immaturity or ignorance. We can be too slow in giving up the reins to the young. "They have to pay their dues!" we think. We tend to view with suspicion anyone who is more powerful or richer or of higher rank—*but younger*—than we.

But what we can't see from our limited perspective is what God has been doing on the inside. That worker in the field doesn't know—doesn't have the slightest idea—what has gone on before in Joseph's life, nor is he even aware of his years in the dungeon. He doesn't know about Joseph's faithfulness when nobody else was around.

Joseph has been appointed, chosen, selected, prepared, and refined into gold by Almighty God. That's how he has come to wear the ring. That's how he has come to get the robe, the necklace, and the chariot. That's why others are saying, "Bow the knee." Joseph himself isn't saying that; others are.

I wonder what Joseph was thinking at that moment?

I believe he was saying to himself over and over, "Praise be to God." I think he was tallying up all the things God had taught him in the past thirty years, things God also wants to teach us.

First: *During the waiting period, trust God without panic.* Count on Him to handle the cupbearers of your life, the people who forget you, the people who break their promises. It's God's job to deal with the cupbearers of your past. It's your job to be the kind of servant He has designed you to be. Be faithful during the waiting periods of life. God will not forget you or forsake you.

Second: *When the reward comes, thank God without pride.* Only God can bring you through and out of the dungeon. Only God can reward you for your faithfulness. If He has, be grateful, not proud. Sure, there will always be some who will find a reason to say that you're not deserving, that you're not qualified for reward or promotion. But you remember, with humility, that it is God who has put you there.

G. Frederick Owen wrote this of Joseph:

> An attempt at seduction; a diabolical plot; base ingratitude; the prison with all its attendant horrors. Yet his unimpeachable manliness, his faithfulness in doing the right, his loyalty to the God of his fathers brought the young man into the palace—he became governor of the land of the Pharaohs.[2]

Some of you are on the verge of promotion and you don't even know it, because God doesn't announce His appointments in advance. What you have to do, while you wait, is to believe His promises. While in the darkness of your dungeon, by faith, trust him to bring the light of a new dawn. In the winter of your discontent, believe there'll be a spring.

The late Joe Bayly, in *The Last Thing We Talk About*, tells of losing three sons, Danny, John, and Joe—each lost at a different age and under different circumstances to death, one before he was five, with leukemia. Remembering those heartaches, Bayly writes of hope finally returning:

> One Saturday morning in January, I saw the mail truck stop at our mailbox up on the road.
>
> Without thinking, except that I wanted to get the mail, I ran out of the house and up to the road in my shirt sleeves. It was bitterly cold—the temperature was below zero—there was a brisk wind from the north, and the ground was covered with more than a foot of snow.
>
> I opened the mailbox, pulled out the mail, and was about to make

a mad dash for the house when I saw what was on the bottom, under the letters: a Burpee seed catalog.

On the front were bright zinnias. I turned it over. On the back were huge tomatoes.

For a few moments I was oblivious to the cold, delivered from it. I leafed through the catalog, tasting corn and cucumbers, smelling roses. I saw the freshly plowed earth, smelled it, let it run through my fingers.

For those brief moments, I was living in the springtime and summer, winter past.

Then the cold penetrated to my bones and I ran back to the house.

When the door was closed behind me, and I was getting warm again, I thought how my moments at the mailbox were like our experience as Christians.

We feel the cold, along with those who do not share our hope. The biting wind penetrates us as them. . . .

But in our cold times, we have a seed catalog. We open it and smell the promised spring, eternal spring. And the firstfruit that settles our hope is Jesus Christ, who was raised from death and cold earth to glory eternal.[3]

The God of Joseph will stay beside us during the dungeon days; He will not forsake or forget us. He will be there during the blast of the winter storm, holding out the promise of springtime. He will be there through the darkest night, quietly reminding us of the promise of morning light.

Many long years ago I made a very important decision in my life. I was wrestling with the question of whether or not God authored the Bible, and I came to the settled conviction that He did, and that therefore this Book was worthy of my trust. With that, I decided to trust God's Word without reservation.

About the same time, I really began studying the Scriptures, and I discovered something amazing: God talked about stuff that I lived with daily! In His Word, He discussed things that I wrestled with personally, problems

I was trying to struggle through on my own—and He offered me answers that worked. And when those answers were not forthcoming, He offered me hope to wait. I decided that His Book was true and absolutely reliable, even when I couldn't see the other end of the tunnel.

The more I studied the Scriptures, the more I realized that its truths fall into various categories. For example, God talks about salvation throughout His Book. He talks about how to come to know Him personally, how to relate to Him intimately. He also talks about forgiveness and what to do with sin. He talks a lot about character traits such as gentleness, patience, goodness, kindness, and joy. But of all the categories of the Bible that I began to take seriously, I think the one that means the most to me falls into the category of the promises. Promises such as,

> As many as received Him [Christ], to them He gave the right to become children of God, even to those who believe in His name.
>
> John 1:12

> Be anxious for nothing, but in everything by prayer and supplication with thanksgiving let your requests be made known unto God. And the peace of God, which surpasses all comprehension, shall guard your hearts and your minds in Christ Jesus.
>
> Phil. 4:6–7

A number of years ago, somebody counted the promises in the Bible and totaled up 7,474. I can't verify that number, but I do know that within the pages of the Bible there are thousands of promises that grab the reader and say, "Believe me! Accept me! Hold on to me!" And of all the promises in the Bible, the ones that often mean the most are the promises that offer hope at the end of affliction. Those promises that tell us, "It's worth it. Walk with Me. Trust Me. Wait with Me. I will reward you for that waiting time. Your gold is being refined."

Joseph learned that a broken and contrite heart is not the end, but the beginning. Bruised and crushed by the blows of disappointment and unrealized dreams, he discovered that God had never left his side. When the affliction ended, he had been refined and he came forth as gold. He had become a person of greater stability, of deeper quality, of profound character.

God's promises are just as much for us as they were for Joseph. His grace is still at work. His tender mercies accompany us from the pit to the pinnacle.

CHAPTER FIVE

Reaping the Rewards of Righteousness

I received a letter the other day that mentioned a survey taken of people who are over ninety-five years of age. They were asked one open-ended question they could answer any way they wished.

"If you could live your life over again, what would you do differently?"

Numerous responses were given. Among all the answers, three were most prominent:

- I would take more time to reflect.
- I would take more risks.
- I would do more things that would live on after I'm gone.

Since I was so young (!), I wasn't a part of that survey, but had I been, I would have submitted another answer along with those three:

- I would have been more affirming.

How about you? On a scale of one to ten, ten being the best, how affirming and encouraging are you of others? How supportive are you of their accomplishments, their achievements?

A couple of test questions help us with our answer. First, how affirming are we when others are afflicted, unable to produce? When they aren't very winsome or responsive? When they're ill or depressed and laid aside? When they are, in the words of Romans 12:15, "those who weep"? Do you encourage and weep with them? Do you offer affirmation and support to those who are in the throes of various forms of affliction?

Seven centuries ago, a man named Francesco di Pietro di Bernardone realized the intense need to be affirming of those who were hurting. We know this man as Saint Francis of Assisi, and a moving prayer we have come to appreciate is attributed to him:

> Lord, make me an instrument of Your peace. Where there is hatred,
> let me sow love; where there is injury, pardon; where there is doubt,
> faith; where there is despair, hope; where there is darkness, light; and
> where there is sadness, joy. . . .[1]

On a scale of one to ten, do you take the time to comfort and weep with those who weep?

A second test question is even more probing: How supportive are you of those who have been promoted? With those who are, in the eyes and minds of the world, successful? They have accomplished much and are being rewarded for their achievement. Do you rejoice and applaud? Or are these people automatically suspect because they have more than you may ever have.

This second question brings some interesting things to light, doesn't it? I have found that most people can much more readily weep with those who weep than rejoice with those who rejoice. This is particularly true in the area of financial wealth and the accumulation of creature comforts. It's been my observation that many folks are uncomfortable with people who are affluent, even when they have no reason to doubt their integrity or the source of their wealth. The ugly side of human nature kicks in, fueled by envy or jealousy, and criticism tends to flow freely.

Tucked away in the folds of Philippians 4 is a little nugget that speaks directly to this. Paul is addressing the first-century church at Philippi, and while writing about his days of difficulty he mentions the two extremes of his life: times when he was down and times when he was up. He commends the people in that church for being affirming and encouraging during both those extremes.

> But I rejoiced in the Lord greatly, that now at last you have revived your concern for me; indeed, you were concerned before, but you lacked opportunity. Not that I speak from want; for I have learned to be content in whatever circumstances I am. I know how to get along with humble means, and I also know how to live in prosperity; in any and every circumstance I have learned the secret of being filled and going hungry, both of having abundance and suffering need. I can do all things through Him who strengthens me. Nevertheless, you have done well to share with me in my affliction.
>
> Philippians 4:10–14

Look at the extremes. "I know how to get along with humble means," admits Paul, "and I also know how to live in prosperity." We have little difficulty picturing Paul in humble means: earning his own living, making tents, while devoting himself to evangelism and teaching, possibly shivering with malaria along the rugged shores of Pamphylia, enduring sleepless nights, being hungry and often without food or drink, imprisoned in a Roman dungeon for his faith. It is a lot more difficult to picture Paul in prosperity, at least by our standards today. Why? I'll be candid here. There seems to be something more spiritual about the hurting, weeping days and something almost carnal about the prosperous days. Yet, Paul said, "I have learned the secret of being filled and having abundance." He had experienced both and learned how to handle both. There were occasions when that godly man enjoyed "abundance."

I can count on one hand, and have some fingers left over, the number of messages I have heard in defense of promotion, of earthly rewards, or of God-given wealth, but there are shelves of books that attack affluence and riches. Yet what would we do without gifts of abundance? Do you have any idea what condition many churches, parachurch ministries, seminaries, Bible schools, and mission agencies might be in if not for those unselfish men and women who give abundantly out of their prosperity? And while I'm on this subject, I should also mention those in the Scriptures whom God blessed with financial wealth—and used them for His greater glory. Those individuals were as rewarded and significant as those who suffered great need.

Now, admittedly, the test of prosperity can be as daunting as anything we face in this life. J. Oswald Sanders wrote, "Not every man can carry a full cup. Sudden elevation frequently leads to pride and a fall. The most exacting test of all to survive is prosperity."[2]

But what of the person who does survive it, honoring the Lord with his or her wealth? Does the evangelical church today embrace that man or woman? Is there room in the pew for someone who is obviously blessed with this world's goods? Or is that person unwelcome because of envy or jealousy or resentment? We're back to my earlier question, how supportive and affirming are we?

These are important questions to consider as we look at the next stage of Joseph's life.

A QUICK ANALYSIS . . . THEN AND NOW

We can picture Joseph wearing that elegant Egyptian headdress he probably wore. We can picture him as he was living the lifestyle of an Egyptian, which he certainly lived. We can picture him in the court of Pharaoh, where he was second in command. But I'd like you to picture him today in your average evangelical church.

Picture him first when he was in the throes of suffering, rejected by his family, sold into slavery, and falsely imprisoned. I'll guarantee you, his name would be on the church's prayer list. We care about those who are booted out of their homes. We care about those who are mistreated and find themselves in great pain. We are concerned about them. We intercede for them. We often reach out to help them. Yes, Joseph's name would have occupied the top of any prayer list.

A Man Restored

Then, through an interesting chain of events, after being falsely accused, imprisoned, and forgotten for an additional two years, Joseph was brought before the king of the land. There, he interpreted a dream correctly, impressed Pharaoh, and suddenly became powerful and prosperous. Just look at what he was given.

Most Old Testament scholars who write of that era say that the land of Egypt could be compared to no other land in the ancient world, except perhaps Babylon which emerged centuries later in all its splendor. It was a place of remarkable influence, enviable educational advancement, military might, and limitless wealth. And the Pharaoh of that land said to Joseph:

"See I have set you over all the land of Egypt."

Genesis 41:41

A New Position of Authority

Note the pronouns, "*I* have set *you*." As we saw in our last chapter, Joseph didn't manipulate this. He didn't even expect it. That's often the way it is in the life of a successful person. The last thing he or she ever expected was the blessing of God in this measure. Personal prosperity was not of concern to him or her.

Pharaoh said, "Joseph, I am promoting you over the land of Egypt." This means Joseph also had financial authority, operating as second in command under Pharaoh. Remember the scene so vividly portrayed in the Genesis account?

Then Pharaoh took off his signet ring from his hand, and put it on Joseph's hand, and clothed him in garments of fine linen, and put the gold necklace around his neck. And he had him ride in his second chariot; and they proclaimed before him, "Bow the knee!" And he set him over all the land of Egypt.

Genesis 41:42–43

The original Hebrew word here, translated *signet ring*, means "to sink." This was a ring used for sinking an emblem into soft clay. Thus, when invoices were placed in front of Joseph, he simply stamped Pharaoh's seal on each one of them with the ring on his finger. He was given decisive authority and financial power over the land. He became the leader others turned to.

On top of all that Pharaoh clothed Joseph in garments of fine linen, placed a gold necklace around his neck, and ordered him to ride in the chariot immediately behind his own. As they rode through the streets, Pharaoh's retainers shouted, "Bow the knee to Joseph!"

The son of Jacob now had wealth, authority, and power—and he looked like it. He was robed in royal garments, had a sparkling gold necklace around his neck, wore the king's ring, and rode in his own government-issued chariot. People bowed as he drove past. The security detail surrounding him, those bronzed soldiers of Egypt, snapped out the orders, "Get on your knees. Show this man respect. This is Joseph, our prime minister!"

Let's jump back to our world today. What would we think if Joseph were a man from our church and all that happened to him? Would it be difficult to be affirming of that kind of success? Would we look at him with a jaundiced eye, wondering, "How did he get there? What did he have to do to get this kind of influence and power? Who does he think he is, wanting us to bow to him?"

Yet the Scripture never says that Joseph expected people to bow before him. In fact, I tend to think that Joseph must have felt embarrassed at times by all the pomp that accompanied his position. There he was, a man still bearing the scars of slavery, riding through the streets of the city with Pharaoh, seeing people kneel before him. In Paul's words, he now had to "learn the secret of being filled, of having abundance."

A New Name and Wife from Egypt

> Then Pharaoh named Joseph Zaphenath-paneah; and he gave him Asenath, the daughter of Potiphera priest of On, as his wife. And Joseph went forth over the land of Egypt.
>
> Genesis 41:45

Along with all this authority, Joseph was given a new name. Once again, he didn't initiate this. He didn't choose a new name for himself; Pharaoh did, naming him Zaphenath-paneah.

This name carries significance. In the heart of it is the syllable "nath." That doesn't mean anything to us today, but if we had lived then, it would have meant much. Neith was one of the goddesses of Egypt. Thus, Joseph's new name meant "the god speaks and lives"! Joseph was given a new Egyptian name, but since it recognized a pagan god, it was not a name he would have chosen for himself.

He was also given a wife he may never have chosen either. Her name was Asenath. Again, notice that syllable, "nath." His wife's name meant "belonging to Neith," and she was a daughter of an Egyptian priest

Suddenly, Joseph was headline news. Suddenly, he held high visibility. Everything Joseph said or did would be noticed throughout the land.

Plutarch, who lived in the first century and watched the abuse of power among so many of the affluent Romans, wrote, "Authority and place demonstrate and try the tempers of men, by moving every passion and discovering every frailty. . . . No beast is more savage than man when possessed with power." He didn't say that every man who had power was a beast or a savage; he said that power offered that great temptation. All these centuries later, we know that to be true. We see it throughout history, and we see it around us in the world today. Because of this, it is second nature for us to suspect those with power. Yet, they don't all deserve that suspicion. By God's grace, there will always be Josephs. By God's grace, you may be one of them. There will always be those who faithfully endured years of hardship, pain, and loss only to emerge into the sunlight of enormous financial benefits and public authority. But what a price they paid en route! I appreciate the words of Victor Hamilton here regarding Joseph: "Between his being sold and his being promoted thirteen years have elapsed—thirteen years of nightmare, hardship, setback and frustration."[3]

Those with power or affluence face more than temptation. Often, they have the disadvantage of being public figures, and when you are a public figure, you can rarely win! You pay a price to become one—and sometimes an even greater price once you're there.

I remember a classic line from Johnny Carson, back when President Reagan was still in office and Carson still reigned on late-night television. Johnny quipped, "Ronald Reagan kept his mouth shut all day today. Tomorrow he'll explain what he meant by that." When public figures speak, they can step on any number of land mines. But even when they remain silent, people wonder what they are hiding, what they are not saying.

Consider the beloved evangelist, Billy Graham, a man just about everybody respects and admires. This dear man has to be careful what he says about political figures, a lesson he has learned well, and sometimes painfully, through his own years in the spotlight. All he has to do is inadvertently tip the scales on one side and he's front-page news! As a result, he has been the object of stinging criticism. Why? Well, that seems to be the way it is when God's hand of blessing rests on some people. And you can never convince me that Joseph did not experience some of this himself.

What a responsibility, what a burden, especially for a man who was only thirty years old!

I remember when thirty seemed like the over-the-hill gang to me. Now it seems marvelously young. But youth does not preclude usefulness. In fact, the Bible is filled with youthful people in positions of leadership and influence. David was not even twenty when he was anointed king by Samuel and only thirty when he took office. When Daniel was picked by King Nebuchadnezzar to be one of the top men in his court, Daniel was only a teenager. Josiah was eight years old when he began to reign as king (now there's a scary thought), and the Virgin Mary was still in her teen years when she bore the Christ child.

In more recent times, Charles Haddon Spurgeon took the pulpit in New Park Street Chapel at age twenty. They built the London Tabernacle to handle the crowds that came to hear him preach. It was filled to capacity before he turned thirty. The people of London stood in the snow outside that church, waiting for the doors to open. The fine expositor, G. Campbell Morgan was only thirteen when he preached his first sermon, and by the time he was twenty-three, some called him "the Bible teacher of Britain."

Compared to some of those folks, Joseph's an old man. *He's thirty!* And he's at the top, with his signet ring, gold necklace, and garments of linen, riding in his chariot, and enjoying his new wife. He has gone from the pit to the palace, from the dungeon to the throne room. And, thankfully, he handled it with humility.

Despite all that, of course, the externals are not what count. What matters is what's on the inside. We don't respect a man or a woman—at least we shouldn't—because of the clothes they wear or the jewels they own or the car they drive or even because they pull a high rating on a public-opinion poll. We respect them because of who they are inside. Integrity has a way of silencing the critic.

Two Sons and a Clear Conscience

God guided the writer of Genesis to reveal the truth about most every area of Joseph's colorful life. He allows us to see what the man was really like inside, even what he was thinking. We can sum it up in one sentence: His heart was humble before God. How do we know? Consider the following:

> Now before the year of famine came, two sons were born to Joseph, whom Asenath, the daughter of Potiphera priest of On, bore to him. And Joseph named the first-born Manasseh, "For," he said, "God has made me forget all my trouble and all my father's household." And he named the second Ephraim, "For," he said, "God has made me fruitful in the land of my affliction."
>
> Genesis 41:50–52

Why does the writer add these details? First, I think he wants us to know that Joseph was monogamous. He didn't fall into the trap of polygamy, like so many surrounding him—even his own family. He had one wife, and she bore him two sons. Second, and more importantly, the writer wants us to realize the significance found in the names of Joseph's sons. Both names are a play on words. The New International Version footnotes state, "*Manasseh* sounds like and may be derived from the Hebrew word for *forget*," and "*Ephraim* sounds like the Hebrew for *twice fruitful.*"

In naming his sons as he did, Joseph proclaimed openly that God had made him forget all his troubles, even those in his father's household.

Above and beyond that, God had made him fruitful in a land and in circumstances that had brought him nothing but trouble. How humble of Joseph to acknowledge that!

The first name, Manasseh, is from the Hebrew root *nashah,* which means "to forget." By naming his first son Manasseh, Joseph was saying, "God has made me forget." How delighted he must have been at the arrival of his firstborn! Perhaps he smiled, standing alongside Asenath, as he gripped her hand and looked into the tiny dark eyes of his son and said, "God has *Manassehed* me—he has removed the sting from my memory."

By naming his second son, Ephraim, another play on a word from the original, meaning "twice fruitful," he was saying, "God has *Ephraimed* me. He has given me two sons. He has blessed me beyond measure in a place that once seemed to bring only suffering."

Joseph gave his children names that would reveal his humble attitude before his God, tagging these boys with reminders of God's activity in his life. "*God* has made . . ." he said. "*God* has given me . . ." he acknowledged.

We all know that in our brains there are places where memories are permanently etched. We do not really forget anything. Sometimes we can't recall it, but it's stored there, nevertheless. Yet Joseph said, "God made me forget."

Ah, that's the point. The memories were still there, lodged deep in the creases beneath his cranium, but when relief finally came, God made him forget the pain, the anguish of what had happened. We know the memories are still there, because later he talks about them with his brothers, as we will see. But God made him get beyond what I would call "the stings" in his memory. So Joseph said, "I named this boy Manasseh because he represents the removal of 'the sting' of yesterday." All this is not unlike the words of the ancient prophet, Joel, who wrote of the Lord's ability to "make up to you for the years . . . the swarming locust has eaten, the creeping locust, the stripping locust, and the gnawing locust" (Joel 2:25).

There is a warning here for all of us. It is very tempting to try to get revenge on the Reubens and the Judahs and the Dans and the Mrs. Potiphars from our past lives. To get back at those who have stung us and stripped us and gnawed on us with evil deeds and ugly words. Instead, we must give birth to a Manasseh. Could it be that it's time to ask the Lord God to erase the stings in your memory? *Only He can do that.* Then it will be time to go on to give birth to an Ephraim. To remember how God has abundantly blessed us. Talk about a positive, affirming name: "God has made me fruitful." But it doesn't stop there. With the plural ending, this word conveys the idea of double benefit—multiple blessings. It's what we would call "superabundance." And it was God who did it all.

I'm reminded of that magnificent line from Paul's letter to the Romans, ". . . but where sin increased, grace abounded all the more" (5:20). I love Eugene Peterson's rendering of that same section of Scripture. He writes: "But sin . . . doesn't have a chance in competition with the aggressive forgiveness we call *grace*. When it's sin versus grace, grace wins hands down."[4]

I've never met a person who truly understood and embraced grace who also continued to hold a grudge. That "aggressive forgiveness" removes the stings and replaces them with waves upon waves of gratitude to God. So it was with Joseph at the births of his two sons.

And what did Joseph do with all the abundance?

Food Amidst Famine

> When the seven years of plenty which had been in the land of Egypt came to an end, and the seven years of famine began to come, just as Joseph had said, then there was famine in all the lands; but in all the land of Egypt there was bread. So when all the land of Egypt was famished, the people cried out to Pharaoh for bread; and Pharaoh said to all the Egyptians, "Go to Joseph; whatever he says to you, you shall do." When the famine was spread over all the face of the earth, then Joseph opened all the storehouses, and sold to the Egyptians; and the famine was severe in the land of Egypt. And the people of all the earth came to Egypt to buy grain from Joseph, because the famine was severe in all the earth.
>
> Genesis 41:53–57

As we have seen, Joseph has been given authority. He holds the keys to the vast vaults of food. He is the master of abundance in the midst of famine.

If I read these verses correctly, this was a widespread famine such as the world had never known, for it says, "The famine was spread over all the face of the earth."

In these circumstances, what did Joseph do? He didn't hoard the storehouses of plenty for himself and his family, or for the royal household, or even for the land of Egypt. He opened those great vaults and released the contents to anyone who needed food. "The people of all the earth came to Egypt to buy grain from Joseph." This was a man who never took advantage of his privileges, his authority, or his financial resources.

With God's help, Joseph foresaw what would happen, but he never took personal advantage of this knowledge. During those seven years of plenty he proved himself faithful. He never took advantage of his power. With quiet and brilliant efficiency, he stockpiled sufficient food to handle the years of famine that were sure to come. Thus, after seven years of prosperity, Pharaoh could still say, "Go to Joseph. He has proven himself worthy of my trust. Go to him. He'll tell you what to do. If you are wise, you will do whatever he says."

Author and pastor Gene Getz does a splendid job of summing up Joseph's management skills:

> At age thirty, Joseph could never have handled this world-class task without an intensive and experience-oriented course in management. It began in Potiphar's house, where he managed all of his affairs. It continued in prison where he was eventually responsible for all the prisoners. And thirteen years later, he was "put . . . in charge of the whole land of Egypt" (41:41).
>
> God's plan for Joseph was on schedule. His preparation was tailor-made for the task God had for him. And because Joseph passed each test, learned from each experience, and learned to trust God more, he was ready when God opened the door of opportunity. He handled prestige and power without succumbing to pride. He persevered with patience and performed his duties faithfully and successfully. He was well prepared.[5]

Evaluation and Application

Well, on a scale of one to ten, how are you doing? Put Joseph in a business suit. Put him in a powerful career position. Dress him in expensive clothes and place him in a huge, beautifully appointed home. Give him a limitless budget and almost limitless power, a luxurious company car, a lovely wife with two healthy sons, and large stock holdings in the food industry. Will you still affirm him? Still stand behind him?

Don't forget, now, he is continuing to walk humbly before his Lord. He has earthly power, but his integrity is still in place, and he freely shares his abundance with others in need. That helps in our evaluation, doesn't it? We cannot help but admire those who reap the rewards of righteousness because God prospers them, when they, in turn, provide for others in need.

I want to go on record here and state that I personally believe that some of the choicest saints in the family of God are those who have walked in integrity as God has blessed them with wealth by His grace, and they use it for God's glory. Ministries I have been a part of have benefited immensely not only from those who have little of this world's goods, but also from the Josephs of this and previous generations. I thank God upon every remembrance of the few in both categories I have had the privilege of knowing.

As we glance back over the previous painful years of Joseph's life, then affirm the rewards God poured into his lap, I find some helpful principles applicable to our own day. Three easily emerge.

First, *lengthy afflictions need not discourage us.* Remember, Joseph was seventeen when he was thrown into the pit and began his long journey through affliction. As we have observed, nothing seemed fair or all that fruitful during the years of the swarming locust. He was thirty years old before he stood before Pharaoh and things began looking up in his life. Pause and consider—from ages seventeen to thirty—thirteen *long years.* Thirteen years since the bottom dropped out of his life. Thirteen years before things changed for the better. Thirteen years of ups and downs, but mostly downs, going from bad to worse. Thirteen years of one setback after another.

Yet read those sections in the Genesis account and try to locate any sign of discouragement on Joseph's part. I have done that. In fact, I have read it aloud, I have read it in several translations, I have even read it in the original Hebrew language, and I cannot find any sign of discouragement. The only possible *hint* of it comes when Joseph tells his two fellow prisoners his story, mentions his innocence, and asks the cupbearer to remember him. Even then, it seems to be only a fair request, given the situation.

Joseph was a man who lived above the drag of despair. He lived far above his circumstances. His long period of affliction did not discourage him.

Second, *bad memories need not defeat us.* Now, I know, it's one thing to say that; it's something else entirely to live it. Speaking personally, I can tell you that I have some memories in my life that are bad memories. If I chose to do so, I could write a book about nothing but difficult people I have encountered, hate mail I have received, and ugly rumors I have endured. But, why would I do that? God has "Manassehed" and "Ephraimed" me! Why live in the swampy, slimy backwaters of bad memories? I have chosen not to let all those locusts sting me or defeat me. If I can learn how to do that, you can too. Let's release all those negatives!

You and I choose what will hold us hostage. We make a choice about who is going to hold us under their thumb. We can often decide who and what will depress us. There isn't a person reading this who doesn't have a store of painful memories that could absolutely defeat you. But they need not. You may need help in turning the wound into a stingless scar. You may need a friend, a mate, even a professional counselor to come alongside to help you in the process of getting rid of those stings. Learn this wonderful lesson with me: We do not need to be defeated by bad memories.

Third, *great blessings need not disqualify us from service.* For too long there has remained a shadow of suspicion over those whom God has chosen to prosper, rather than a thankful response that says, "Praise God! Here is an individual who has been raised up by God for His glory, to be used in places I could never reach! May his prosperity abound and may his unselfish generosity increase. May his ear never be closed to the hurting." Modern-day Josephs are needed just as much today as the original Joseph was needed in the ancient history of Egypt.

I love to read the old, classic authors. One of my favorites is a Scottish preacher and writer named Alexander Whyte who served forty-seven remarkable years in the same church in Edinburgh. In his fine volume *Bible Characters*, he writes this of Joseph.

> Joseph was now to be plunged into the most corrupt society that rotted in that age on the face of the earth. And had he not come into that pollution straight out of a sevenfold furnace of sanctifying sorrow, Joseph would no more have been heard of. The sensuality of Egypt would have soon swallowed him up. But his father's God was with Joseph. The Lord was with Joseph to protect him, to guide him, and to give him victory. The Lord was with him to more . . . promotion; to more and more honour, and place, and power, till this world had no more to bestow upon Joseph. And, through it all, Joseph had become a better and an ever better man all his days. A nobler and an ever nobler man. A more and more trustworthy, and a more and more trusted and consulted man. More and more loyal to truth and to duty. More and more chaste, temperate, patient, enduring, forgiving; full of mind and full of heart; and full, no man ever fuller, of a simple and a sincere piety and praise of God, till he became a very proverb both in the splendour of his services, and in the splendour of his rewards.[6]

To the Josephs that God is raising up in this generation and the next, may you continue to walk with Him. May you generously use your affluence and authority for His glory, and your influence and success to make His Word and truth known. The Christian is not always afflicted, not always the object of hatred and persecution. Some, by the grace of God, are thrust into roles of honor and leadership. How we need such leaders!

Remember, though, the message of Jesus Christ cuts across all strata of status and success. It doesn't make any difference what your salary or lifestyle is, what car you drive, where you live, or where you work. All of those factors have a lot to do with your position before people, but they have nothing to do with your position before God. And sadly, I have found that among the most affluence there is often the greatest poverty, among the fullest coffers there is often the greatest emptiness, the greatest spiritual void. Not always—but often.

God *can* use our authority and our abundance and our promotion as He did with Joseph. But before He can, we need to humble ourselves before God's mighty hand and say, "Jesus Christ, I need You. I have all of this to account for, and I can't take any of it with me. Please use me as you see fit." With authority comes the need for *accountability*. With popularity comes the need for *humility*. With prosperity comes the need for *integrity*. Joseph passed all three tests with flying colors.

Those who model the same depth of character mixed with wisdom deserve our respect and affirmation.

CHAPTER SIX

Activating a Seared Conscience

I'm thinking of a few lines from Gilbert and Sullivan's comic opera, *Mikado*. At the beginning of one of their typical rollicking songs, there are lyrics that always evoke spontaneous laughter, as one of the performers mentions a list of offenders—the kinds of people who could be dispensed with and who never would be missed! Funny, isn't it? Everyone in the audience quickly responds—because everyone in the audience has a little list of folks who have hurt them and deserve retribution.

It's time for a few more penetrating questions, which only you can answer. Are you the kind of person who keeps "a little list"? Do you remember what you would be better off forgetting? When someone has done you wrong, do you allow the Spirit of God to erase that offense? Or do you cling to a grudge, secretly add their name to your list, and wait for that choice opportunity to strike back?

Those were the questions Joseph faced—and answered correctly.

A FAMINE IN CANAAN

As we pick up his story, you'll remember the situation. A worldwide famine had struck. The situation was dire, and people were starving.

The only country that had food was Egypt. Because of God's hand on Joseph, the Egyptians had been forewarned so that they could prepare for the lean years—under Joseph's leadership. Now starving people from other lands had begun to trickle into Egypt begging to buy food.

Meanwhile, the Spirit-directed camera of Holy Scripture leaves Egypt and adjusts its zoom lens on a hamlet in Hebron back in the land of Canaan. Back in the place of Joseph's childhood, which he was forced to leave over twenty years ago.

> Now Jacob saw that there was grain in Egypt, and Jacob said to his sons, "Why are you staring at one another?" And he said, "Behold, I have heard that there is grain in Egypt; go down there and buy some for us from that place, so that we may live and not die."
>
> Genesis 42:1–2

Joseph's father and brothers were still alive, but they were not doing well; their homeland had been devastated by the famine. It was during that time the old patriarch Jacob heard that there was grain in Egypt.

"Why are you sitting around looking at each other?" he said to his sons. Can't you hear the old fella? When you reach his age, patience gives way to pontification. "Why are you sitting here twiddling your thumbs. We need food. We're starving. The cisterns and wells have dried up. Our crops are withered. The land is barren. We've had no rain and no relief for months. We need help. I understand there's food in Egypt, so I want you to get yourselves down there and bring some back. If you don't, we're all going to die."

Jacob sent all of his sons off to Egypt—all except his youngest son, Benjamin, the one remaining child of his long-deceased Rachel. Jacob kept him at home.

Remember now, back in Canaan, Jacob thought Joseph was dead, and Joseph's brothers knew nothing of his whereabouts. "Who cares? Out of sight, out of mind" best describes their attitude.

> . . . the sons had become middle-aged men, with families of their own. They probably never mentioned that deed of violence to each other.

> *They did their best to banish the thought from their minds.* Sometimes in
> their dream they may have caught a glimpse of that young face in its
> agony, or heard the beseechings of his anguished soul; but they sought
> to drown such painful memories by deep draughts of the Lethe-stream
> of forgetfulness. Conscience slept.[1]

They certainly didn't know that the brother they sold into slavery some
twenty or more years earlier was now prime minister of Egypt. All they knew
was that they had to obey their aging father and bring back food.

Meanwhile, back at the ranch, Joseph knew nothing about his family.
Surely, in unguarded moments, alone with his thoughts, he must have
wondered about their welfare. Was his dear father still living? Were the
brothers all alive; were they well? Had the famine taken its toll on them?
While he was busy with his life in Egypt, carrying out his responsibilities
as prime minister, his thoughts certainly returned to those simpler days of
yesteryear. His main activity at this time was seeing that the people were
fed, and overseeing the distribution of the food in storage to many outside
Egypt who came with hope for relief.

All of this sets the stage for what has to be one of the most remarkable
and dramatic stories in history. To this day, it touches chords of great emotion in audiences the world over as the scenes are reproduced on film and
in live-theater productions.

ENCOUNTER IN EGYPT

> So the sons of Israel came to buy grain among those who were coming,
> for the famine was in the land of Canaan also. Now Joseph was the ruler
> over the land; he was the one who sold to all the people of the land.
> And Joseph's brothers came and bowed down to him with their faces
> to the ground. When Joseph saw his brothers he recognized them, but
> he disguised himself to them and spoke to them harshly. And he said
> to them, "Where have you come from?" And they said, "From the land
> of Canaan, to buy food."
>
> Genesis 42:5–7

Let your mind imagine that! All ten of the older sons of Jacob—Reuben, Simeon, Levi, Judah, Issachar, Zebulun, Gad, Asher, Dan, and Naphtali—are ushered into the presence of the prime minister of Egypt. The surroundings must have seemed awesome to these country boys from Canaan as they stood before the prime minister, a man of immense authority and wealth who, by controlling the world's food, held the power of life and death in his hands. We can see how overwhelmed they were, because the initial response of the group was to bow down "with their faces to the ground." Keep in mind, they had no clue that the Egyptian, robed in royalty, was their long-lost brother.

On the other hand, look at it from Joseph's perspective. At this point, he may have been exhausted. First there had been the stress of building the granaries, as well as planning and rationing during the years of plenty; now there was the pressure of having to dispense Egypt's stored grain with prudence, equity, and wisdom. Every day he faced his own people, plus a parade of people from foreign lands, including this latest travel-worn, rather ragtag bunch of Hebrews. Since he instantly recognized them and realized they failed to recognize him, he enjoyed a classic opportunity rarely allowed a person with his power, given their sordid past. Talk about one's moment! Well, at least they bowed respectfully before him. Then, as they stood up and he looked into their faces, he watched them carefully.

They were bearded, unlike the usually clean-shaven Egyptians. They wore the garb of Canaan and spoke the language of his people, the Hebrews. Joseph must have peered at them intently, studied them with his eyes, listened as they spoke, perhaps trying to discern each one's identity. There was no question; these men were his brothers! (*I love scenes like this!*)

I have often wondered whether, perhaps, Joseph had been looking for them all along. As the people of other countries poured into Egypt seeking food, he may have wondered whether someday his own family might appear before him.

Finally, there they stood—and the account tells us "he recognized them, but he disguised himself." There's a play on words here in the Hebrew. They were *recognized*, but he made himself *unrecognizable* (disguised himself). He went beyond that, in fact, for it says he "spoke harshly to them."

"Where have you come from?" the Egyptian prime minister barked out sharply.

There was no reason for them to recognize him, of course. Many years had passed. He was clean-shaven. He wore the headdress of Egypt. He spoke to them in Egyptian through a translator. In the eyes of Jacob's ten sons, he was only an intimidating and powerful official.

Since Joseph recognized them and realized they did not recognize him, he had to think fast. The absence of any bitterness freed his mind to think creatively—even playfully. And what had been an interesting exchange became exceedingly significant.

> When Joseph saw his brothers he recognized them, but he disguised himself to them and spoke to them harshly. And he said to them, "Where have you come from?" And they said, "From the land of Canaan, to buy food."
>
> But Joseph had recognized his brothers, although they did not recognize him. And Joseph remembered the dreams which he had about them, and said to them, "You are spies; you have come to look at the undefended parts of our land."
>
> Genesis 42:7–9

"Why are you here?" he asked them.

"We've come to buy food," they said. "We are from the land of Canaan, and we're starving there."

Suddenly Joseph experienced a divinely appointed déjà vu. While he was standing there talking to his brothers, the dust of twenty years blew away from his memory and he remembered his own dreams of long ago.

He recalled his brothers' sheaves of wheat bowing before his sheaf, and the sun, moon, and eleven stars bowing down to him. How tempting it must have been to reveal himself at that moment and remind them of those dreams. Those dreams for which they had mocked him and hated him! How self-satisfying it would have been to say, "I told you so!" Instead, Joseph decided to buy a little time.

"You've come to spy on us," he accused them. "You've come to assess the areas of our country that are not well-defended so that you can attack us and steal our food."

"No, no, no," his brothers protested. "We are hungry from the famine. We have simply come to buy food."

Now, watch closely and see this unusual dialogue unfold:

> "We are all sons of one man; we are honest men, your servants are not spies." Yet he said to them, "No, but you have come to look at the undefended parts of our land!" But they said, "Your servants are twelve brothers in all, the sons of one man in the land of Canaan; and behold, the youngest is with our father today, and one is no more." And Joseph said to them, "It is as I said to you, you are spies; by this you will be tested: by the life of Pharaoh, you shall not go from this place unless your youngest brother comes here!"
>
> Genesis 42:11–15

Put yourself in Joseph's sandals. How must he have felt as he heard their words? So far as his brothers were concerned, he no longer existed! He was buried in the graveyard of their memories. He was "no more." Out of sight, out of mind, gone forever.

Three times Joseph accused them of being spies. Then, in one of their responses, they unwittingly gave him information he wanted. They told him that his father and Benjamin were still alive! By mentioning them, the brothers also played into Joseph's hand.

"There is one way you can prove your innocence, prove you are telling the truth," Joseph told them. "You can bring me your youngest brother. But I still don't trust you, so only one of you can go. The rest will be imprisoned here as hostages."

Then, after proposing this plan, Joseph put all of them in prison for three days. We're told nothing of what transpired during those three days. It is left to our imagination. On the third day, however, for some reason, he revised the plan, offering to keep only one of them as a hostage. The rest could return to Canaan to bring back their younger brother, Benjamin.

Now Joseph said to them on the third day, "Do this and live, for I fear
God: if you are honest men, let one of your brothers be confined in
your prison; but as for the rest of you, go, carry grain for the famine
of your households, and bring your youngest brother to me, so your
words may be verified, and you will not die." And they did so.

Genesis 42:18–20

We don't know why Joseph changed his plan or what he was hoping
to accomplish with all this, but we can imagine what was surging through
Joseph's mind: "I wonder if Benjamin is healthy and strong? And what
about my father? Is he too old to remember? Oh, how I long to see my
entire family. How tempted I am to tell them who I am—they'll be shocked!
What I really wonder about is the condition of their hearts."

Joseph chose Simeon as hostage and had him put in shackles there in
his brothers' presence. Why did Joseph pick Simeon? We might think he
would have chosen the firstborn, but that was Reuben, who had tried to save
Joseph's life back at the pit when they all teamed up against him. Perhaps
Joseph remembered Reuben's attempt to intervene on his behalf, and instead
chose the second eldest brother, Simeon, to remain behind.

Before he did that however, he listened in on a conversation among his
brothers, as they spoke in Hebrew to one another, thinking he could not
understand. Remember, as part of his disguise Joseph had been communi-
cating with his brothers, speaking in Egyptian through an interpreter. But
Joseph understood every word.

In this exchange, we see how a seared conscience can be activated and
begin to be revitalized.

Then they said to one another, "Truly we are guilty concerning our
brother, because we saw the distress of his soul when he pleaded with
us, yet we would not listen; therefore this distress has come upon us."
And Reuben answered them, saying, "Did I not tell you, 'Do not sin
against the boy'; and you would not listen? Now comes the reckoning
for his blood." They did not know, however, that Joseph understood,
for there was an interpreter between them. And he turned away from

them and wept. But when he returned to them and spoke to them, he took Simeon from them and bound him before their eyes.

Genesis 42:21–24

In the original language, the "we" in their conversation is emphatic! "*We* are guilty . . . *we* saw the distress of his soul . . . *we* would not listen. . . ."

The first step toward activating a seared conscience is *taking responsibility for one's own personal guilt.* The brothers did not blame their father for being passive. They did not blame their brother Joseph for being proud or arrogant or favored. They did not diminish the wrong by saying they were too young to know any better. They used the right pronoun when they agreed together, "*We* are responsible! There is no one else we can blame!"

> Whatever they may have said in prison, now at least they speak in terms of their guilt in the matter of Joseph. Their conscience has awakened mightily during these three days. They feel that a just retribution has come upon them, and are apparently all of one mind in regard to the matter. They admit guilt, the "only acknowledgment of sin in the book of Genesis."[2]

Notice also that they talked about a transfer of distress. "We ignored the distress of his soul when he pleaded with us and we put him in the pit and then sold him into slavery. We can still see those eyes. His face comes back to haunt us." The original Hebrew root of distress means "to bind, to restrict, to cramp, to tie up." Not the kind of binding used to shackle Simeon, but theirs was an emotional binding.

When you have done wrong to someone and haven't gone through the necessary process to make things right with them and with God—when you haven't fully dealt with your transgression—you become the victim of the very distress that you put that person through. "We feel the same distress that we caused him and saw in his face."

Do you remember Edgar Allan Poe's short story *The Telltale Heart?* In it the murderer couldn't sleep because he kept hearing the beating heart of his victim down in his basement; he wasn't hearing the victim's heart, of course; he was hearing his own heart, pounding in his chest, reverberating through his skull. His own guilt awoke him, and it finally led to the revelation that he was the murderer.

The brothers' crime was now more than two decades old, but they still felt the distress of it. Time doesn't erase distress. We have evidence of that in our own lives. We know from experience the inescapable reminders of our guilt. The emotional entanglements brought about by the consequences of our own sin can be so devastating that we become physically sick, which is precisely what happened with David following his adultery with Bathsheba and his murderous plot to have Uriah, her husband, killed. Remember his heartsick admission?

> When I kept silent about my sin, my body wasted away
> Through my groaning all day long.
> For day and night Thy hand was heavy upon me;
> My vitality was drained away as with a fever-heat of summer.
>
> Psalm 32:3–4

Eugene Peterson puts it this way: "The pressure never let up; all the juices of my life dried up."[3]

I wonder what Joseph felt when he heard his brothers' words, when he heard them admit their guilt over what they had done? We are told he had to leave the room so he could weep. What tears of relief and joy! He understood well one of the reasons they were breaking. They had been in the dungeon for three days, and he knew what that was like. He had spent years in a dungeon. He knew what that could do to a person. He also knew that when God comes to tap on stooped shoulders and to break a guilty heart, He does not stop with a slight nudge or mild reproof.

St. Anne of Austria, a sixteenth-century saint, once wrote, "God does not pay at the end of every day, but at the end, He pays."

The long-outstanding bills were coming due for Joseph's brothers. And as their debt rose ever higher before their eyes, they openly admitted, "We are guilty!"

Many years ago, an able preacher named William E. Sangster concluded a message on Joseph with this true story.

> It was Christmas time in my home. One of my guests had come a couple of days early and saw me sending off the last of my Christmas cards. He was startled to see a certain name and address. "Surely, you are not sending a greeting card to him," he said.
>
> "Why not?" I asked.
>
> "But you remember," he began, "eighteen months ago . . ."
>
> I remembered, then, the thing the man had publicly said about me, but I remembered also resolving at that time with God's help, that I had remembered to forget. And God had "made" me forget.
>
> I posted the card.[4]

William Sangster did not keep a list. Neither did Joseph. Part of the reason we know that is that he named his son Manasseh, whose name meant "God has made me forget." Every time Joseph called his boy's name it was a reminder that he had covenanted before God to get past the sting, to forget what his brothers had done to him.

Now those brothers stood before him, and he saw them beginning to break. "We are guilty," they said. "What we did was wrong, and the distress of our brother has been transferred to us."

In tune with God's timing, Joseph did not reveal himself to them. Instead, he retained Simeon as a hostage and sent them on their way to Canaan with distinct instructions to bring back Benjamin.

Before they left, however, Joseph performed an act of grace.

> Then Joseph gave orders to fill their bags with grain and to restore every man's money in his sack, and to give them provisions for the journey. And thus it was done for them. So they loaded their donkeys with their grain, and departed from there. And as one of them opened his sack to give his donkey fodder at the lodging place, he saw his money; and behold, it was in the mouth of his sack. Then he said to his brothers, "My money has been returned, and behold, it is even in

my sack." And their hearts sank, and they turned trembling to one another, saying, "What is this that God has done to us?"

Genesis 42:25–28

Joseph's brothers wanted to get out of Egypt, like, fast. When the sacks of grain they had bought were loaded on their donkeys, they immediately began their journey back to Canaan. But something happened on the first night they stopped to rest and feed and water the animals. When one of the brothers opened a sack to get food for his donkey, he saw that the money he had given to the prime minister of Egypt was tucked into the top of the bag.

"I can't believe this!" he exclaimed. "Look! My money has been returned. It's here in the sack."

The other brothers quickly opened their sacks and discovered that their money had been returned to them also.

Instead of being happy about this surprise, however, they were frightened. "Their hearts sank, and they turned trembling to one another. . . ." The original word that is translated "trembling" is the same word used in 1 Samuel 14:15 to describe a giant earthquake. It's also used in Genesis 27:33 to describe the trembling of Isaac when he learned that his son Jacob had stolen Esau's birthright. In fact, we read there that Isaac "trembled violently." He shook, literally! And that's what Joseph's brothers began to do. They began to shake. They began to tremble as they looked at one another. And then they said, "What is this that God has done to us?"

I love that statement. Not only are they now feeling the full brunt of their own guilt, they are also sensing God's hand in this. "What is God doing?"

When God activates a seared conscience *we begin to gain a different perspective.* Sometimes we become victims of the kind of treatment we have meted out to someone else. When the harm, the hurt, or the pain that we brought on someone else is visited upon us, something begins to change inside us. God begins to break through our hard shell and soften our hearts that had become calloused.

These brothers had no idea that Joseph was still alive. All they knew was that they were going through great distress and it instantly—I mean *instantly*—reminded them of the distress they had caused their brother over twenty years earlier.

Again, the passing of time does not erase a guilty conscience. The ache lingers . . .

- even after everyone in the family grows up;
- even after the crime is dismissed in the courtroom;
- even after the divorce is final and you have walked away . . . without biblical justification;
- even after the things done in secret are far from anyone's awareness;
- even after decades of polluted water have washed beneath the bridge of memory.

There is distress. There is that "telltale heart" thumping in your chest. This is part of the breaking of the will, the softening process that begins to activate one's once-seared conscience.

God also activates a seared conscience *when we are recipients of undeserved expressions of grace*. Joseph's brothers deserved no grain. They deserved no money. They deserved punishment, perhaps even imprisonment, for what they had done to their brother. Instead, they wound up with freedom, a full sack of grain, and all of their money returned.

They deserved to be on Joseph's hit list, but Joseph didn't have such a list. Remember the cupbearer? Joseph had been in prison two extra years because, at least humanly speaking, the king's cupbearer had forgotten him. The man he had helped and encouraged had forgotten him in an instant. Then, suddenly, Joseph was released, and he eventually became the most powerful man in the land of Egypt apart from Pharaoh. What an opportunity to take revenge against that cupbearer in Pharaoh's court. But he didn't. In fact, we don't find Joseph ever speaking one word of resentment against the cupbearer.

Why? Because Joseph walked with God. He refused to spend his days asking, "Why did he forget me?" He prayed, in effect, "God, get the process done. I'll keep my eyes on You. I'll accept being forgotten. Keep my heart right. And when the moment comes, may I speak for Your glory. If You ever choose to use me again, may I revel in Your grace and release all feelings of resentment and revenge."

Now we have seen him, at least thus far, respond that very way with his brothers. Not only did he not retaliate against them, he demonstrated grace with an abundance of mercy.

A FINAL REMINDER

Are you still keeping a list? Perhaps part of the reason you still nurture it is that God has not yet brought you into a similar circumstance. Perhaps you have not yet seen how abundantly His grace has rearranged and restored your life.

Through the years I have noticed that people who keep lists tend to have an insensitivity toward God; they allow a thickness, a callousness of heart to continue. What a dreadful way to live—and die!

If that has happened to you, I want to invite you to come to the cross of Jesus Christ, who once for all removed our names from the list of the unforgiven. Though we haven't earned His favor, though we deserve death, He has given us life.

How grateful we should be that the telltale heart is still at work. It is God's work of convicting us, bringing us to repentance. His Spirit does not stop working with us even when we stop being interested in Him. It represents the central-most place in our lives, where He is leading us back into harmony with Himself. Your response—your choice to obey His voice—will change the rest of your life.

The insightful words of C. S. Lewis provide an appropriate conclusion to this soul-searching chapter:

> Every time you make a choice you are turning the central part of you, the part of you that chooses, into something a little different from what it was before. And taking your life as a whole, with all your innumerable choices, all your life long you are slowly turning this central thing either into a heavenly creature or into a hellish creature:

either into a creature that is in harmony with God, and with other creatures, and with itself, or else into one that is in a state of war and hatred with God, and with its fellow-creatures, and with itself. To be the one kind of creature is . . . joy and peace and knowledge and power. To be the other means madness, horror, idiocy, rage, impotence, and eternal loneliness. Each of us at each moment is progressing to the one state or the other.[5]

CHAPTER SEVEN

Groanings of a Sad Dad

Murphy's Law says, "If anything can go wrong, it will." If you wash your car on Saturday morning, it will rain on Saturday afternoon. If you go to bed early, the phone will ring. If you drop a piece of bread you have just spread thick with peanut butter and jelly, it will always fall peanut-butter-and-jelly-side down. If you take your troubled car to the mechanic, it will run perfectly once you are at the shop.

When things are going well, something *will* go wrong—just wait. When things just can't get any worse, they will. Anytime things appear to be going better, it's just because you have overlooked something. No matter which way you ride your bicycle, it's always uphill and against the wind. If you fiddle with a thing long enough, it will break. The other line always moves faster.

NATURAL TENDENCIES IN ALL OF US

Because life often doesn't work out right—which being interpreted, means, it doesn't work out *our* way—we have developed three basic and very natural tendencies.

First, *we tend to respond negatively rather than positively.* When circumstances begin to turn against us or when life becomes a larger challenge than we can see our way through, our immediate reaction or response is negative instead of positive. This is especially true when facing unexpected changes. Unless you are different from most, your first reaction is *no.*

Second, *we tend to view problems horizontally rather than vertically.* By this I mean that we view problems strictly from a human point of view. We tend to leave God out of the picture until we have our back against the wall in an absolutely impossible situation. Only then do we bring in the vertical. And sometimes not even then.

Third, *we tend to resist what is new, especially if it seems too good to be true.* We resist rather than embrace—especially when it is something that appears to be exciting and full of new opportunities. Stop and think. When was the last time you showed no resistance to the possibility of a move? Can't remember? Neither can most of us. We focus on what "can't happen" instead of on what might. We think, rather, about leaving the familiar, stepping into an uncertain situation, and running the risk of disappointment. I realize the need for wise appraisal and careful planning, but isn't it interesting that our first response to something new is usually resistance? I know—I've been there dozens of times in my adult life.

These three tendencies seem to intensify as we grow older. Rather than getting better, we get more brittle. There is greater fear of danger—a fearful hesitation rather than an openness to living positive Christianity. By "positive" I don't mean living in a dream world, being gullible and undiscerning, but living with our eyes wide open. I don't mean pumping up what is wrong and calling it right; I mean realistically seeing God in the crucibles and the casseroles of life. That is not only possible, it is preferred. I am finally realizing that is the way to live. And I'm loving it alongside a wife who is even more risk-taking and courageous than I! We're the Harley-ridin' couple, remember?

JACOB'S RESISTANCE AND RELUCTANCE

Jacob, Joseph's father, didn't live like that. He was a man who really had trouble walking by faith, even though he had known the Lord for well over a hundred years. Jacob wrestled constantly with suspicious negativism, a horizontal viewpoint, and a closed, resisting mind. We shall soon see it again.

The Return and Report

When we pick up the story, Jacob's sons have finally made their way back to Canaan. They have rehearsed their experiences in Egypt and reported to Jacob their encounter with the prime minister. And, of course, they mentioned the fact that their brother Simeon has been kept there as a hostage until they return with their youngest brother, Benjamin. This was the patriarch's choice opportunity to turn everyone's attention to Jehovah. Could He be at work in this? Did He have a plan—some kind of marvelous, unexpected opportunity—before them? They must trust in Him!

But, alas, not so! Watch Jacob's response:

> And their father Jacob said to them, "You have bereaved me of my children: Joseph is no more, and Simeon is no more, and you would take Benjamin; all these things are against me." Then Reuben spoke to his father, saying, "You may put my two sons to death if I do not bring him back to you; put him in my care, and I will return him to you." But Jacob said, "My son shall not go down with you; for his brother is dead, and he alone is left. If harm should befall him on the journey you are taking, then you will bring my gray hair down to Sheol in sorrow."
>
> Genesis 42:36–38

The Discussion and Debate

When Jacob learned what had happened, the old gentleman shriveled in fear. Rather than saying, "Thank God, He is at work. Men, He loves us and watches over us. In His care we are all safe," he responded negatively and horizontally.

His sons had not only returned with the food they needed, but also with all of their money. They had been given grain from Egypt free of charge. All the prime minister had asked was that they prove they were not spies by returning with their youngest brother and claiming Simeon who had been left as a hostage. Yet Jacob saw none of this as God's provision. He froze in fear and focused on a worst-case scenario. His response was negative and horizontal.

His sons had the same tendency. Remember, they were "dismayed" when they found the money. The brothers had responded negatively, out of suspicion, just as their father did now.

Incidentally, the original word here, from which "dismayed" is translated, is the same word used in Genesis 3:10 to describe Adam's reaction after he had sinned and was hiding from God: "I heard you in the garden, and I was *afraid* . . . so I hid" (NIV).

Sometimes we need to be afraid, especially when we have been in the wrong. I read a true story several years ago about a man and a woman who stopped at a Kentucky Fried Chicken place to pick up some supper. They bought two chicken dinners and took them to a picnic area. But when they opened the bag, they found a lot more than chicken. There were bundles of money inside the bag!

Honest guy that he was, the man drove back to KFC and returned the money. The manager was ecstatic as he explained what had happened. He had been working in the back and had put all of the day's proceeds in one of the chicken take-out bags and set it aside, ready to go to the bank. When the woman working the counter had reached over to get their order, she accidentally grabbed the wrong bag.

The manager was so impressed with this man's honesty that he said, "I'm going call the local newspaper and have them come over and get a photo of you two. Folks need to know there are still honest people around."

"No, don't do that," said the guy. He pulled the manager aside and whispered in his ear, "I'm married . . . and the woman I'm with is not my wife."

Sometimes folks should be afraid when the money shows up! But this was not one of those occasions. Jacob should have been thankful his sons were still alive. They had been accused of being spies and could have been killed on the spot. Besides having their lives spared, they had been given the food they needed and had their money returned. All they had to do was return and show the prime minister of Egypt that they really did have a younger brother, that they had been telling the truth.

But Jacob not only reacted negatively and horizontally, he overreacted. As soon as he heard they had left their brother in Egypt, he jumped to the conclusion that Simeon was dead. "Joseph is dead. Simeon is dead. Everything is against me," he moaned. He began to sound paranoid and self-pitying. "All these things are against me!"

Last time I checked, Jacob was supposed to be the patriarch of the clan, the spiritual leader. Yet, with a quick glance behind the scenes, as we sneak a peek through the back door of the tent, we see Jacob as he really is. He's a negative, close-minded, horizontal-thinking man who's pulling his hair out in fear. "Where is God in this?" he whined. "Everything is against me!"

At that point, Reuben intervened once again and said, "Hey, I'll make you a deal, Dad. You may put my two sons to death if I don't bring Benjamin back to you."

But Jacob said, "No. You cannot take my son down there with you. His brother, Joseph, is dead, and he is the only one I have left. If anything should happen to him, I would die."

It's amazing, but it's as if his other sons don't even exist. It's as though he doesn't include the two younger men, Joseph and Benjamin, with the other ten. It's as though they are a separate entity and not nearly as precious. "These two brothers . . . my sons," he calls them. He doesn't call them "*your* brothers." Sounds to me like a father sowing seeds of favoritism again. How must Reuben and the others have felt when their father said, "I only have *one son* left"?

"If I let you take him down there and something happens to him, I will go to my grave heartbroken," Jacob said. Fatalism reigned supreme in the old man's heart. How tragic!

It's one thing for us to sit with this book in hand and read the story, knowing what the outcome will be, and say with a shrug, "I'll tell you this, I sure wouldn't have done that. I would have trusted God if I had been in that situation." But would you really? Well, then why didn't you trust Him last week? What was it that kept you from seeing God's hand in that matter you couldn't handle last month? Call to mind your most recent major test. Did you rest calmly in Him? Or did you push the panic button out of fear?

Negative thinking. A horizontal viewpoint. A closed mind to something that is unexpected and new. That's why we tend to panic. Because, humanly speaking, you and I have been programmed toward defeat. We have formed habits of response that leave God out of the picture. We don't actually announce it in those words, we just model it and rationalize around it by calling it something else. And aren't we relieved God didn't put our biography into print?

Yet here the Spirit of God hides nothing. He shows us the side of Jacob that is all warts—the ugly side that we all have.

Another way to analyze the impact of the man's response is to realize that at this point Jacob was a grandfather and probably a great-grandfather, perhaps a great-great-grandfather. He was a *patriarch* who should have been saying to his sons, "Boys, things may seem bleak, but this is the time to trust in God's sovereign promises. We need to call some of them to mind. He will provide! Benjamin, let's get on our knees, and let's pray for your safety, and let's watch God work. There's a reason He put that money in those sacks. There's a reason He wants you to go down to Egypt. We don't know what it is yet, but we'll trust Him for the answer."

Instead, Jacob reacted with fear, suspicion, paranoia, negativism, and pride. "Nope," he said. "No way. Benjamin is not going."

Does that sound familiar? We get just enough information to be dangerous and then we make a hurry-up decision. We find ourselves sitting way out on a limb, as our pride saws off weak branches of faith. We can't admit we've made a mistake, a bad judgment call. To make matters worse, we spread those germs of fear through our family or our company or our church. And then we dig in our heels with stubborn determination.

"Never!" said Jacob. His pride was at stake. To renege now would make him look weak. There's no way he can back down now; he's delivered his soul and thrown down the gauntlet. He went on record to say, "Absolutely not!" Little did he realize he would soon be eating those words.

Since confession is good for the soul, then it's time for me to come out of hiding and tell you that I can identify, in many ways, with Jacob's initial horizontal reaction. I, too, have had to eat my own words. My thoughts take me back to a phone call I received over five years ago. I was engaged in a pastoral ministry many would consider enviable. For well over twenty years the Lord had poured out His blessings. Everything was working—great staff, outstanding board of lay leaders, wonderful music ministry, numerous and splendid support groups, a youth ministry many wished to copy, familiarity with my surroundings, favor with the people, and a dozen more benefits I could name. God's grace, I can assure you, was abundant.

That phone call represented an invitation for me to leave that place of service—and all the familiarity, friends, and family we had nurtured for more than two decades—and begin anew in a completely different role at a totally different place with an entirely different group of people. From a church to a seminary. From a pastoral role I'd cultivated for more than thirty years—the shepherd of a flock—to a presidential role I'd never even dreamed of. From the known to the unknown. From California to Texas. From a home we had lived in all that time, to a garage apartment I'd occupy until we could settle in a home almost eighteen months later. No thanks! I couldn't say no fast enough. In fact I said, *"Absolutely not!"*

So emphatic was I that I wrote a two-page letter spelling out, in no uncertain terms, all my reasons. It was an airtight, carefully crafted written defense, leaving no room for any question. As I looked at the future there really was no way I could even consider such a change. Certainly not at my age or stage in life. I mean, were those people crazy? My letter was mailed—and that was that.

Only one problem, *I was wrong.* To be blunt about it, I resisted rather than remaining open.

To the point: Everything within me wanted to cling to the familiar, to keep things simple and uncomplicated, to stay where I was, finish well, and ride off on our roaring bike into the sunset with a big smile on my face and Cynthia perched behind me. But God had another arrangement, and the changes have been even more than I expected. But we are *exactly* where

He wants us, doing *exactly* what He planned for us, accomplishing *exactly* what He had in mind way back when I was laughing at the whole idea and saying, "There is no way!" And we're having the time of our lives.

Do I understand Jacob's initial reaction? *Absolutely, yes!*

JACOB'S FINAL ACCEPTANCE

Interestingly, God gets His way. He always does, but it's a lot more painful when we fight Him and resist His leading, based on negative thinking, horizontal perspective, and resistance to change.

First, *Jacob denied and delayed.*

> Now the famine was severe in the land. So it came about when they had finished eating the grain which they had brought from Egypt, that their father said to them, "Go back, buy us a little food." Judah spoke to him, however, saying, "The man solemnly warned us, 'You shall not see my face unless your brother is with you.' If you send our brother with us, we will go down and buy you food. But if you do not send him, we will not go down; for the man said to us, 'You shall not see my face unless your brother is with you.'"
>
> Genesis 43:1–5

God was at work, and as a result, the famine didn't abate. Months after Jacob's sons had returned with the grain from Egypt, they were once more in serious trouble.

"That's it. That's all the grain. The last sack is emptied, Dad." (I'm smiling here as I watch God tighten the screws in order to get His way. Little did Jacob know that his resistance would be so temporary. Been there, done that.)

"Okay," said Jacob. "Go back to Egypt and buy us more food."

"We can't go back there unless we take Benjamin," said Judah. "The head man down there warned us not to come back without him." But Jacob was in denial, still unwilling to face reality. He had refused to hear this when his sons first told him, and he had been denying it for months, refusing to lift a hand to return for his son Simeon. He simply resigned himself that Simeon was lost forever, like Joseph, and thus delayed any response.

Then, when Judah tried to shake his father out of his denial and delay, Jacob responded with *blame and deceit.*

> Then Israel said, "Why did you treat me so badly by telling the man whether you still had another brother?"
>
> Genesis 43:6

Jacob leveled this petulant charge, and once again turned everything back on himself. "Why did you do this do me? Why did you bring this trouble on me? Why did you even tell that man that you had another brother?"

Remember, Jacob's name and nature meant "deceiver," so we're not surprised that the pattern emerged yet again. "Why didn't you just lie? Why did you tell him the truth?"

Proverbs 12:22 tells us that "Lying lips are an abomination to the LORD, but those who deal faithfully are His delight."

Jacob's response, when cornered, was to lie. When his back was against the wall, he was still willing to be deceitful. Is it any wonder that his sons had done the things they had? Their father had taught them by example that there were times when you had to twist the truth a little. "Who cares that a lie is an abomination to the Lord? Why did you ever tell him you had another brother?"

But something had happened, however small, to the seared consciences of his sons. Now several of them joined in, trying to get Jacob to listen and understand. If he wouldn't do what was right before them, then they decided to level with their father.

"Listen, Dad," they said:

> "The man questioned particularly about us and our relatives, saying, 'Is your father still alive? Have you another brother?' So we answered his questions. Could we possibly know that he would say, 'Bring your brother down'?"
>
> Genesis 43:7

Parents, please listen to this. Sometimes your children are in very difficult straits and they attempt to convey to you their concern and anxiety. But you, in anger and pride, stop listening. Instead, you begin to pontificate about some solution to the problem. You begin blaming and moralizing before you have even heard all the facts.

I'm not proud of my rebellious years. Thank God they weren't many and they weren't that severe, but I do remember them. I remember when they started—when I sensed my parents were no longer listening to me. I was not a rebel at heart, but down underneath I had a lot of things churning around, and I really *did* want to confide in my parents. Yet when I tried, I felt one or both would cut me off before I could even finish. My sentences were finished for me, and my struggles were misconstrued as rebellion. In my case, I just backed away. The distance grew, and it was not until many years later I felt the closeness again—after I was a parent, rearing my own children.

Jacob's sons were simply trying to set the record straight, to get their father to see the truth. "Dad, we were standing there in front of Pharaoh's right-hand man and he specifically asked us if our father was still living and if we had another brother. So we told him the truth. 'Yes,' we said. We had no idea why he was asking."

Then Judah made an offer. Remember, the famine had not eased and the situation was getting desperate. They had many mouths to feed.

> And Judah said to his father Israel, "Send the lad with me, and we will arise and go, that we may live and not die, we as well as you and our little ones. I myself will be surety for him; you may hold me responsible for him. If I do not bring him back to you and set him before you, then let me bear the blame before you forever. For if we had not delayed, surely by now we could have returned twice."
>
> Genesis 43:8–10

Judah put it on the line. "You can't continue to delay and deny the situation. I'll take responsibility for Benjamin's life. If anything happens to him, I will bear the consequences for the rest of my days. Come on, Dad, let's cooperate. If we hadn't delayed this long, we could already have been down there and back twice with food."

Judah offered to take the blame, even though blaming is a futile exercise. Yelling at darkness doesn't make it light. But we like to blame. "Dad," said Judah, "if you want to blame somebody, blame me. But let Benjamin go. Man, we're dying here."

So Jacob reluctantly gave in. He responded with what I would call *tolerance and uncertainty*. First he denied and delayed. Then came blame and deceit. And now, finally, tolerance and uncertainty. He was one tough nut to crack!

> Then their father Israel said to them, "If it must be so, then do this: take some of the best products of the land in your bags, and carry down to the man as a present, a little balm and a little honey, aromatic gum and myrrh, pistachio nuts and almonds. And take double the money in your hand, and take back in your hand the money that was returned in the mouth of your sacks; perhaps it was a mistake."
>
> Genesis 43:11–12

Perhaps his response went something like this: "Oh, all right. If you have to do it, then here's the procedure I want you to follow." See his attitude? And then he reverted to another old pattern. He ordered them to take gifts, things that were native to Canaan. If he had lived in the days of Solomon, he would have claimed Proverbs 21:14: "A gift in secret subdues anger, and a bribe in the bosom, strong wrath."

Years before, he had done that with his brother, Esau, and it had worked. It might work with the Egyptian prime minister too.

Jacob could see all kinds of schemes, but he still refused to see God's hand at work. He could not say, "Look, boys, we don't know what all this means, but we do know that we're confused and we need God's help. Let's trust God for protection and insight on this. Let's ask Him to give us direction on what to do."

Parents, this is an appropriate time for me to urge you to call your families to prayer. "Hey, kids, let's pray about this before we leave the breakfast table."

Or, "Let's spend some time Saturday morning asking God for direction in this situation. We don't know what to do." Maybe one of your sons or daughters is edging into rebellion. Listen to them. Listen longer than normal. Try hard not to butt in. Admit it when you're not sure how to respond. Then sit down and pray together, asking for God's direction.

Jacob never did that. Even in his best moment, up till now, he was saying, "Maybe it was a mistake and we'll win his favor with a gift."

Finally, though, he made some movement toward *a guarded faith and abandonment.* His own hunger pangs persuaded him to resist no longer.

> "Take your brother also, and arise, return to the man; and may God Almighty grant you compassion in the sight of the man, that he may release to you your other brother and Benjamin. And as for me, if I am bereaved of my children, I am bereaved."
>
> Genesis 43:13–14

Just when you think, *There he goes; that's the patriarch in action; that's our model,* Jacob says, "Take Benjamin and go, and may El Shaddai go with you and give this Egyptian compassion toward you so that he will spare Simeon and Benjamin. As for me—poor me—if none of you come back, I'll just have to live with it." We've just read the groanings of a sad dad.

Jacob said too much. If only he had ended his farewell speech with ". . . Benjamin." No self-pity. No whining. No "woe is me" sniffling. Then those sons of his could have left with "El Shaddai" ringing in their ears and thinking *God Almighty will grant compassion. God Almighty will provide, just as our father reminded us!* But no, Jacob, again, took the low road. As one man put it, "It [Jacob's final comment to his sons] is a statement of resignation, of a willingness to accept the worst possible scenario."[1]

> So the men took this present, and they took double the money in their hand, and Benjamin; then they arose and went down to Egypt and stood before Joseph.
>
> Genesis 43:15

I wonder what those ten men, those ten grown sons of Jacob, talked about during that journey from Canaan to Egypt? I have an idea that it might have been the same things we would have talked about had we been in their sandals. I also believe these men were beginning to be broken. Perhaps, they spoke of how much they missed their brother, Joseph. With Benjamin now among them, maybe they felt this was a good time to express their sorrow over their past actions and, together, sincerely request El Shaddai's power and protection. I so want to believe that God was starting to melt their hearts before Him! In fact, that's the beauty of this story as it progresses. We're led to wonder what exactly they were thinking. We so desperately want to get to the end to see the happy ending, but we must wait. Because there's always something to learn along the way.

A RETURN TO THE ORIGINAL AXIOMS . . .
AND SOME COURSE CORRECTION

When we're on our journey from Canaan to Egypt, we tend to be negative rather than positive. We tend to view life horizontally rather than vertically. We tend to be resistant rather than open to that which is new and unexpected. As a result, we are, more often than not, reluctant, suspicious, closed people. When we are threatened by the unexpected, we put up our defenses. Or we raise the paranoia banner: "They're all against me. They don't understand." We need some course-correction techniques to break those habits!

I can think of at least three that have worked for me.

1. *Recognize and admit your negative mentality.* So much of the cure is in the confession. Immediate correction begins with honest admission. Recognize, realize, admit your negative mentality. Don't hide it. Quit denying it. It will help if you and I simply say, "I have fallen into the habit of negative thinking."

2. *Force a vertical focus until it begins to flow freely.* I have never seen a habit just lie down, surrender, and die; we have to make

a conscious effort if we hope to break longstanding habits. If you are negative today, chances are very good that when you wake up tomorrow morning you're still going to be negative. In fact, you'll be even better at it tomorrow morning because you'll have perfected it for one more day. So force a vertical focus. That means first, you pray for strength. Then you make a conscious effort to respond, "Could God be in this? Is God trying to get through to me?" Or, "How would You, Lord, right now, react to this?" Or, "Lord, I'm not sure what to do, I admit that my tendency is to keep You at a distance. That's a response from my flesh. I invite You to come and help me deal with this. Give me clear direction, the answer that would please You, or the strength to wait. But I want to see You in all of this." That's forcing a vertical focus.

3. *Stay open to a new idea for at least five minutes.* Don't try it for an entire day, because you'll almost panic. Just take on your day five minutes at a time. When something new, something unexpected, confronts you, don't respond with an immediate "Nope! Never!" Wait five minutes. Hold off. Tolerate the possibility for five minutes. You could be surprised at the benefit of remaining open those three hundred seconds.

I have no idea where this hits you today. But I do know this: Life is full of changes and challenges, both of which can be difficult to face. They can also be hard to handle with a positive, vertical mentality. Rather than telling another story that illustrates the benefits of such a response or quoting a page full of verses that emphasize the value of trusting God instead of resisting change, I want to pause at this place in the book and pray. These are my words, but I'd like you to see yourself in them.

> *Lord God:*
> *I have no way of knowing who is reading my words today or what he or she is going through at this time in life. But I do know this: You are still*

El Shaddai. The God of unlimited might, boundless power, overwhelming strength. No obstacle formed against You can hold You back. No one intimidates You and nothing is too hard for You. Furthermore, since You know the end of the story—Joseph's story, as well as our story—You have the ability to work everything out, so we have no reason to fear.

But we're only human. That means we tend to be negative, horizontally focused, and intolerant of new ideas. However, we have come to the place in our lives where we are sick and tired of those tendencies. We need Your El Shaddai strength to help us break those habits and we need Your El Shaddai might to face the future courageously.

With Your help, we start today. Give us fresh hope to think positively, to trust in Your sovereign control over everything we shall encounter. Calm our fears. Give us fresh courage and a strong confidence in You. Make us contagiously enthusiastic as we begin this new way of thinking and living. Turn our focus from the horizontal to the vertical. Help us to grow old gracefully, saying, "Yes" to life's challenge and "I'm open" to life's changes.

I ask this in the all-powerful name of Jesus Christ.

Amen.

CHAPTER EIGHT

Fear Displaced by Grace

When the Iron Curtain was drawn across Europe after World War II, people felt trapped. We began hearing incredible stories about people who had escaped the Communist regimes and were then reunited with their families in the West. Occasionally the evening news would flash a poignant picture of that emotional moment when family members saw each other for the first time after years of forced separation. Always, that reunion defied description, and a picture truly was worth a thousand words: the catching sight of the arms thrown open wide, the running to one another, the embrace that did not want to let go, the dancing, the screaming, the tears of joy.

In a similar way, none of us who saw it will ever forget the scene at Clark Air Base in 1973 when 143 brave men stumbled out of an airplane—some bent, some crippled, but all of them returning prisoners of war, now freed from the prisons in North Vietnam. The highest ranking soldier on board that first flight, forty-eight-year-old Naval Captain Jeremiah Denton, a prisoner for nearly eight years, stood before the microphone and, with quivering voice, said, "We are honored to have had the opportunity to serve our country under difficult circumstances. We are profoundly grateful to our commander in chief and to our nation for this day." After a brief pause, he managed to say, "God bless America!" Then he and the others who had been flown to freedom fell into the arms of their waiting families.

Words fail to convey the emotion of such scenes. Merely imagining them can bring tears to our eyes. I mean this in the right sense when I say that such scenes are almost too emotional to analyze objectively—too sacred to watch. There stand family members who have lived on memories and spent literally hours in the throes of concern, wondering if they would ever see each other again. As life went on while they were separated, not a day passed without their hearts returning to one another. And then, there they were together again—struggling to put those years of separation into words. As songwriter, Fanny Crosby once put it, "Chords that are broken . . . vibrate once more."

A scene not dissimilar from those I have just described is about to occur in our story of Joseph. Again, the emotions that surround it are difficult to put into words as all the brothers of a family, separated for more than two decades, will soon be united.

EN ROUTE FROM CANAAN TO EGYPT—AGAIN

As we begin this segment of Joseph's story, Simeon is still being held hostage in Egypt, and Jacob's other sons are returning to that land with their youngest brother, Benjamin. Their mission is fourfold: to show their good faith, to prove they are not spies, to ransom Simeon, and to buy more food. They are also bringing back the original money that had been returned to their sacks on their first visit; in fact, you may remember they have brought double that amount, along with several special gifts. Finally they arrive, full of questions and concerns. *Will the Egyptian prime minister release Simeon? Will he look with favor on us for returning the money, or will we all be imprisoned like our brother? Will he let us return?*

These men were trembling with anxiety. They didn't know what awaited them in Egypt. They didn't know if they would ever find Simeon or if he was still alive. They had no idea what would happen when they once again stood before the royal ruler.

> So the men took this present, and they took double the money in their hand, and Benjamin; then they arose and went down to Egypt and stood before Joseph.
> When Joseph saw Benjamin with them, he said to his house steward, "Bring the men into the house, and slay an animal and make ready; for the men are to dine with me at noon." So the man did as Joseph said, and brought the men to Joseph's house.
>
> Genesis 43:15–17

Guilt plagued these sons of Jacob. It weighed heavily on their shoulders and whispered in their ears. On more than a few occasions they had relived what they had done to their younger brother Joseph over twenty years earlier. All the recent events to and from Egypt had pricked their conscience. They remembered, but still, they had not yet fully repented of their evil ways. But they would. Oh, yes, they would.

FEARFUL BROTHERS WITH JOSEPH'S STEWARD

Our story quickly shifts from the worried brothers to the eager and excited Joseph awaiting their return. Unknown to them, Joseph looked out at his brothers through eyes of remembrance—but from a distance. At long last he was relieved to witness their return to Egypt. He had probably been waiting and watching, wondering if they would accept his challenge or leave Simeon to his own fate, as they had him so many years before. But finally they returned. Joseph forced himself to stay calm.

Banquet Plans

Counting their number, he realized Benjamin was with them. *So that's Benjamin,* he thought as he stared at his younger brother. How Joseph's heart must have pounded in his throat when he saw this man who had been just a lad when Joseph was wrenched from his family.

It's time for us to have that feast, he said to himself, then ordered his steward to have a meal prepared and to bring the men from Canaan to his home.

I have often wondered what Joseph's steward thought about all this. It must have seemed strange, to say the least. Why would the prime minister invite this dusty, dirty tribe of Hebrew nomads to a feast? But the steward obeyed his master. He had the banquet prepared, as ordered, and brought the Israelites to Joseph's house.

Uneasy Explanation

> Now the men were afraid, because they were brought to Joseph's house; and they said, "It is because of the money that was returned in our sacks the first time that we are being brought in, that he may seek occasion against us and fall upon us, and take us for slaves with our donkeys." So they came near to Joseph's house steward, and spoke to him at the entrance of the house, and said, "Oh, my lord, we indeed came down the first time to buy food, and it came about when we came to the lodging place, that we opened our sacks, and behold, each man's money was in the mouth of his sack, our money in full. So we have brought it back in our hand. We have also brought down other money in our hand to buy food; we do not know who put our money in our sacks."
>
> Genesis 43:18–22

By now, all these grown men were really beside themselves with fear. What was going on? Their own guilt magnified their anxiety. Unresolved guilt *always* magnifies anxiety. *It must be about the money,* they thought. And so they began stumbling over themselves, trying to explain to the prime minister's bilingual servant.

William Shakespeare, in *King Henry VI*, wrote, "Suspicion always haunts the guilty mind."[1] If you are feeling guilty over some wrong you have done, everything that happens begins to play into that, causing apprehension and suspicion to pulsate. *They are going to find out.*

Notice what Joseph's brothers feared: "He may seek occasion against us and fall upon us, and take us for slaves." They had sold their own brother into slavery, and now that was what they feared for themselves. Paralyzed by guilt, they feared *the worst*, when Joseph dominated by grace, was planning *the best*.

Guilt causes us to say strange things at strange times. I remember reading about a letter that had actually been mailed to the Bureau of Internal Revenue. "Dear Sir:" it began. "I haven't been able to sleep because last year when I filled out my income tax report I deliberately misrepresented my income. I am enclosing a check for $150." Then came the closing line, "If I still can't sleep, I'll send you the rest." That's partial response to unresolved guilt.

Dr. Paul Tournier, a man skilled in medicine and wise in the ways of faith, wrote an entire book on *Guilt and Grace*. In it, he wrote these insightful thoughts about feelings of guilt:

> The public generally does not realize how much torment the majority of doctors suffer, nor how much worry they must have over a case; they are in a perpetual state of alertness: Did I overlook some useful point in my examination? Did I make a mistake in diagnosis? Is there some effective method of treatment unknown to me or that I have not thought of? They mull it over in their minds to the point of obsession.
>
> Similarly with the parents of a child who is the victim of an accident. Questions crowd into their minds. They weigh the circumstances of the drama, which such a little thing might have obviated. They remember some little fact that they might have taken as a presentiment, but which they didn't bother about.
>
> It may seem brutal to say so, but there is no grave beside which a flood of guilt feelings does not assail the mind.[2]

Anyone who has dealt with death as much as a pastor does would have to agree that Tournier is right. Beside the grave you often see guilt written across the faces of the grieving. Could I have done more? Did I do too little? Was that decision right? If I had done something differently, would he have lived longer? Suffered less? Though not graveside guilt, these now-grown men wrestle with similar struggles.

Guilt always does a number on us. It certainly did on Joseph's brothers. Though, standing before an unnamed, soft-spoken servant from Egypt, whom they had never really known throughout their lives, they poured out their confession.

"We don't know how the money got back in our sacks the first time, but here it is. We've brought it all back. We also brought additional money to buy more food. That's why we're here . . . to buy food."

Calming Response

> And he said, "Be at ease, do not be afraid. Your God and the God of
> your father has given you treasure in your sacks; I had your money."
> Then he brought Simeon out to them.
>
> Genesis 43:23

I love the steward's reassuring response: "Be at ease," he told them. The Hebrew Bible says, simply, "Shalom." The steward, who knew their well-known language, used their word for *peace*. He said, in effect, "Hey, shalom, men—be at peace. Settle down. Don't be afraid." And then this Egyptian even witnessed to them about their God. "Your own God is the one who put the treasure in your sacks. Nobody thinks you stole it. I know what happened; I was the one who put it there. I was the one who had your money. It was a treasure from Elohim, the God of your father."

They were in agony, wondering when the other shoe was going to drop. Instead, the steward said, "Shalom! Elohim has done it again." What a reproof! And, by the way, what an interesting surprise that this Egyptian steward understood some pretty sound theology. No doubt, the result of Joseph's influence through the years. He personifies what we considered in the previous chapter—vertical perspective.

Joseph's brothers had never thought to relate the return of their money to the abundant grace of God. Why? Because *guilt* had kept them from seeing God's hand of grace in their lives. (It always does!) Yet the unmerited favor of God had come in abundance to them: grain in abundance, money in abundance. And now their brother Simeon is restored to them, healthy and whole. Mercy in abundance.

GRATEFUL BROTHERS WITH JOSEPH

Then the man brought the men into Joseph's house and gave them water, and they washed their feet; and he gave their donkeys fodder. So they prepared the present for Joseph's coming at noon; for they had heard that they were to eat a meal there.

Genesis 43:24–25

This strange situation had the sons of Jacob totally confused. They had come bearing money and gifts, hoping to buy the good will of the Egyptian prime minister. More importantly, they had brought Benjamin, as the man requested. Instead of being asked about any of this, however, they had been taken to the prime minister's home for a feast, where they were allowed to refresh themselves, learn a little theology from an Egyptian steward, and then be reunited with Simeon.

Reunion Reestablished

When Joseph came home, they brought into the house to him the present which was in their hand and bowed to the ground before him. Then he asked them about their welfare, and said, "Is your old father well, of whom you spoke? Is he still alive?" And they said, "Your servant our father is well; he is still alive." And they bowed down in homage.

Genesis 43:26–28

Suddenly the prime minister arrived on the scene. They hastened to present their gifts to him. But he was neither angry nor harsh. He was not marching up and down, breathing threats and demanding to see Benjamin. In fact, he seemed overjoyed to see all of them again. Almost immediately he asked about their father. Was the old man still alive? Was he well?

"Yes, yes . . . he's still alive," they replied. "He's over a hundred now, and is still in good health."

Despite the official's good humor, sincere interest, and solicitude, they remained uneasy and anxious, still not knowing what to expect from this powerful man.

Then came one of those rare moments that, as I mentioned at the beginning of the chapter, defy description:

> As he lifted his eyes and saw his brother Benjamin, his mother's son, he said, "Is this your youngest brother, of whom you spoke to me?" And he said, "May God be gracious to you, my son."
>
> Genesis 43:29

Emotions Released

Here we have one of the most eloquent sentences in Scripture: "He lifted his eyes and saw his brother Benjamin."

Joseph looked up and saw his blood brother for the first time in some twenty years. "He saw Benjamin, his mother's son." The only brother to whom he was totally related—same father, same mother. The other boys were really his half brothers, but Benjamin was his full blood brother, his only direct connection with his mother Rachel.

Joseph stood there, tears threatening to well in his dark eyes as he gazed upon that beloved face. "Is this the youngest brother you told me about?" he asked, struggling to maintain his composure.

"Yes, this is Benjamin."

And Joseph said tenderly, "May God be gracious to you, my son."

Suddenly, this great man, this strong-hearted and efficient prime minister of a mighty nation, collapsed inside. Like the rest of us, great men and women encounter those times in life when they can no longer restrain their emotions. Composure flies away and feelings take control. That was what happened to Joseph at this long-awaited moment in time. It is at such sacred occasions words fail us. Often we need to get alone to gain our composure. Joseph did.

> And Joseph hurried out for he was deeply stirred over his brother, and he sought a place to weep; and he entered his chamber and wept there.
>
> Genesis 43:30

Can't you imagine the scene? All of a sudden, the handsome, bronzed leader of millions has rushed to his bedroom and collapsed in sobs. All those years passed in review. All the loneliness. All the loss. All the seasons and birthdays and significant occasions without his family. It was too much to contain, like a rushing river pouring into a lake, swelling above the dam. His tears ran and he heaved with great sobs. All of a sudden, he was a little boy again, missing his daddy.

My thoughts rush to other great men in Scripture who at times were overwhelmed by their emotions.

David, when he lost his precious son Absalom, grieved as he cried out: "O my son Absalom, my son, my son Absalom! Would I had died instead of you, O Absalom, my son, my son!" (2 Samuel 18:33).

Job, who had lost everything, including his children and his health, cried out to God: "Let the day perish on which I was to be born, and the night which said, "A boy is conceived. . . . Why did I not die at birth . . . ? (Job 3:3, 11).

Elijah, after God's great victory against the prophets of Baal on Mount Carmel, got the threatening word from Jezebel that, within twenty-four hours, he would be murdered. "But he himself went a day's journey into the wilderness, and came and sat down under a juniper tree; and he requested for himself that he might die, and said, 'It is enough; now, O LORD, take my life, for I am not better than my fathers'" (1 Kings 19:4).

Even the giants of the faith had times when they simply exploded emotionally before their God.

Consider in greater detail our great spiritual ancestor Moses. He had trekked long miles through the barren wilderness, leading the Hebrews to the Promised Land. Although God had brought them miraculously and safely out of Egypt, the people started complaining as soon as they got across the Red Sea. They were tired of the heat; it never ended. They were tried of the food; it all tasted the same. They were tired of the water; it tasted brackish. They were tired of sand and gravel and endless wilderness. They wanted Egypt with all its comforts. Complain, complain, complain. Grumble, grumble, grumble. Gripe, gripe, gripe.

Suddenly, in an outburst of emotion, Moses said, "Enough! I've had it!"

So Moses said to the LORD, "Why hast Thou been so hard on Thy servant? And why have I not found favor in Thy sight, that Thou hast laid the burden of all this people on me? Was it I who conceived all this people? Was it I who brought them forth, that Thou shouldest say to me, 'Carry them in your bosom as a nurse carries a nursing infant, to the land which Thou didst swear to their fathers'? Where am I to get meat to give to all this people? For they weep before me, saying, 'Give us meat that we may eat!' I alone am not able to carry all this people, because it is too burdensome for me. So if Thou art going to deal thus with me, please kill me at once, if I have found favor in Thy sight, and do not let me see my wretchedness."

Numbers 11:11–15

If you want to get the full effect of Moses' meltdown, go back and read this passage aloud, with feeling. *Imagine!* He's talking to the Lord God here, the Almighty, El Shaddai, himself.

"Did I give birth to all these people? Why do I have to baby-sit them? Where am I going to get meat for all of them? They keep whining that they want meat! I've had it! Just kill me, Lord. Let me out of here . . . put me out of my misery!"

Is that any way to talk to God? You'd think that the Lord would just zap him with a full load of Sinai lightning and thunder. But He didn't.

I have a friend who lost a son. They found the boy drowned at the bottom of the neighbor's swimming pool. My friend and his wife, after the public grief had ended, continued to grieve within. "To this day," I remember his saying, "there are times we have to choke back the feelings."

"Shortly after the drowning," he said, "I got in my car and I drove the Los Angeles freeways for miles. As I did, I lashed out with words that I would never say outside that car. No one else was there, and I just poured out all of my feelings. Grief and resentment, anger and confusion, I dumped it all. After more than two hours of that, I drove back home, pulled into my driveway, and turned off the engine, my eyes and cheeks still wet with tears. I laid my head against the steering wheel, completely exhausted. Then, I suddenly was struck with the thought: *God can handle all this.*"

You know the best part? God will never tell on you. Isn't that great? Isn't it a relief to know that the Lord God will never stand up in church and say, "I am here to announce what she said to Me last Thursday morning?"

There have been times in my own life when I've had doubts, when I've stumbled over great cracks that appeared in my world. I've had those times when I climbed into my own bed and wept, crying out to God, just as you have. Such is life, especially when you decide to be real rather than protect some kind of I've-got-it-all-together image. It's comforting to realize we're in good company in times like that, isn't it?

Joseph was a great and powerful man, admittedly, but he was also a real human being with real human emotions, who could step out of the corridors of power and have the strength to weep his heart out.

And so this sturdy, capable prime minister of Egypt was overcome with emotion when he saw his younger brother for the first time in so many years. The record states, "He was deeply stirred and he sought a place to weep!" Again, a scene that defies detailed description.

And then, rather matter-of-factly, it goes on to say that "he washed his face," got himself under control, and rejoined his brothers and ordered the servants to "serve the meal." I love this next scene.

Fellowship Restored

> So they served him by himself, and them by themselves, and the Egyptians, who ate with him, by themselves; because the Egyptians could not eat bread with the Hebrews, for that is loathsome to the Egyptians.
>
> Genesis 43:32

After the deeply emotional moment, there is almost a little humor, a little comic relief, in this scene. Joseph was eating by himself, the brothers were eating by themselves, and the other Egyptians were eating by themselves. All these folks were sitting down to lunch in the same place, but they were eating at separate tables.

The Egyptians could not bear to eat with the Hebrews. The New International Version study note says: "The taboo was probably based on ritual or religious reasons" and refers to Exodus 8:26, where Moses says to Pharaoh, "'The sacrifices we offer the LORD our God would be detestable to the Egyptians'" (NIV). That helps explain why they were seated at separate tables.

> Now they were seated before him, the first-born according to his birthright and the youngest according to his youth, and the men looked at one another in astonishment. And he took portions to them from his own table; but Benjamin's portion was five times as much as any of theirs. So they feasted and drank freely with him.
>
> Genesis 43:33–34

Author and scholar, Henry Morris, explains the reason behind their astonishment.

> After they were assigned to seats at their table, the eleven brothers noted a remarkable thing. They had been seated in order of age, from the eldest through the youngest. If this were a mere coincidence, it was indeed marvelous. One can easily show . . . that there are no less than 39,917,000 different orders in which eleven individuals could have been seated! . . . Evidently, this man knew a great deal more about their family than they had realized; or else he had some kind of supernatural power. They had no answer, and could only wonder about it.[3]

Joseph's brothers were astonished at the way they were being treated. They had expected any number of things to happen to them, including possible death, but certainly not this. Now here they were, seated according to age, dining with the prime minister. And what a feast! They were served fresh garden salads, thick T-bone steaks, fried okra, overstuffed baked potatoes, cornbread, black-eyed peas, and big glasses of iced tea (if Egypt was anything like Texas)! Besides that, the prime minister unloaded more food from his own table.

Benjamin, interestingly, was served portions five times the size of the other men . . . like, five big steaks, five huge helpings of peas, five giant baked potatoes, five servings of cornbread, five tall glasses of tea! Those hungry Hebrews must have thought they'd died and gone to glory. Benjamin himself may have thought, *I know I'm thin, but this is ridiculous. What's going on here?*

By now Joseph was totally oblivious. *This is Benjamin! My brother!* He was so ecstatic, so overjoyed that he just kept piling on the food. Sounds like something an older brother would do for one he hasn't seen in ages, doesn't it? Especially, when the elder is full of forgiveness and grace!

Amazing, isn't it, how Joseph's acts of grace freed up everyone around the tables. At the outset, there were feelings of anxiety and dread as guilt held them in its clutches. Their fear knew no bounds as they returned to Egypt, wondering what they would face.

Within a brief span of time, they found themselves treated kindly, sitting around a banquet table loaded with food, and, of all things, relaxing in the joyful presence of royalty. What relief! Better than that, what grace! They were the recipients of favor they hadn't earned and kindness they didn't deserve. And they were overloaded with an abundance of provisions they could never repay. Is anyone surprised they were astonished and no longer afraid? Their fear was now displaced by grace. Why? One reason—Joseph. This great man, though not as yet known to them to be their brother, determined to forgive their mistreatment and, instead, demonstrate great grace. Rather than remind them of their wrongs and force them to pay for their cruelty and injustices from years gone by, he showed them favor to the maximum extreme. This reunion was really a banquet of grace—on full display—thanks to Joseph, a man of integrity and forgiveness.

A SIMPLE YET VERY PERSONAL ANALOGY

Joseph's life offers us a magnificent portrayal of the grace of God as He came to our rescue in the Person of His Son, Jesus. So many come to Him, like Joseph's guilty brothers, feeling the distance and fearing the worst from God, only to have Him demonstrate incredible generosity and mercy. Instead of being blamed, we are forgiven. Instead of feeling guilty, we are freed. And instead of experiencing punishment, which we certainly deserve, we are seated at His table and served more than we can ever take in.

For some, it's too unreal. So we desperately plead our case, only to have Him speak kindly to us—promising us peace in our own language. We then try to fend off His anger by bargaining with Him, thinking our hard work and sincere efforts will pay Him back for all those evil past deeds we're guilty of. But to our astonishment, He never even considered our attempts important enough to mention. What we had in mind was earning just enough to silence our guilt, but what He had in mind was overwhelming us with such an abundance we'd realize we can never, ever repay.

What a beautiful picture of Christ at the cross, bearing the sins we committed, forgiving us in the process. Isn't it amazing? The One who was rejected is the same One who works so hard to get us reunited with Him.

> Therefore the LORD longs to be gracious to you,
> And therefore He waits on high to have compassion on you.
> For the LORD is a God of justice;
> How blessed are all those who long for Him.
>
> Isaiah 30:18

Do you long for Him? I've got great news! In an even greater way—greater than you could ever imagine—He longs to be gracious to you. He is offering you all the things you hunger for. The table is loaded, and He is smiling, waiting for you to sit down and enjoy the feast He prepared with you in mind. Have a seat—grace is being served.

Frederick Buechner writes:

> After centuries of handling and mishandling, . . . most religious words have become so shopworn nobody's much interested any more. Not so with *grace*, for some reason. Mysteriously, even derivatives like *gracious* and *graceful* still have some of the bloom left.
>
> Grace is something you can never get but only be given. There's no way to earn it or deserve it or bring it about any more than you

can deserve the taste of raspberries and cream or earn good looks or bring about your own birth. . . .

A crucial eccentricity of the Christian faith is the assertion that people are saved by grace. There's nothing *you* have to do. There's nothing you *have* to do. There's nothing you have to *do*. . . .

There's only one catch. Like any other gift, the gift of grace can be yours only if you'll reach out and take it.

Maybe being able to reach out and take it is a gift too.[4]

CHAPTER NINE

"I Am Joseph!"

Why was Joseph considered great? Why does the Spirit of God hover over his life more than any other person in the book of Genesis, *including Abraham*? What was there about Joseph that could have caused the Lord to say something like this to Moses, the writer of the Pentateuch: "Make a careful record of this man's life so that future generations can spend an extended amount of time with him"?

Joseph certainly wasn't superhuman. He was merely a man. He never walked on water. He had no halo. He never performed a miracle. He certainly wasn't free from trouble. Nor was he an untarnished or untouchable plaster saint. With the Lord's help and by his own admission, he interpreted some dreams, but he made no awesome prophecies. So far as we can determine, he never wrote any holy Scripture.

Then, why was Joseph so great? He was great because of his faith in God, which manifested itself in a magnanimous attitude toward others and his magnificent attitude toward difficulties. A strong faith leads to a good attitude. When those two essentials are in place, troubles become challenges to face not reasons to quit.

Elbert Hubbard, an American writer early in this century, once wrote,

"The final proof of greatness lies in being able to endure contemptuous treatment without resentment." Joseph passed that test with flying colors.

As we pick up his story, we come to what seems to be a rather uneventful incident. In fact, Martin Luther had trouble with Genesis 44 and once wondered why the Spirit of God took the time to preserve such a trivial thirty-four verses." Why indeed. The truth of the matter is that it is in the trivial and mundane details of life that our attitude is tested the most. Most of life is not "super-fantastic"! Much of life is just a cut above toothpaste—just plain, garden-variety, ordinary stuff, not that much to write home about.

Joseph knew this. He had seen his own attitude tested in high places and low, in significant scenes of high drama and down in the dregs of deep despair. But perhaps his greatest test was in the wait of the long haul. He wanted to see in his brothers some of the same attitude that God had kindled within him—a powerful faith in God and a positive response to others. But his brothers still haven't presented much evidence to show that they share Joseph's perspective. So he set up a two-part final exam for his brothers.

THE TEST: SILVER IN THE SACK

> Then he commanded his house steward, saying, "Fill the men's sacks with food, as much as they can carry, and put each man's money in the mouth of his sack. And put my cup, the silver cup, in the mouth of the sack of the youngest, and his money for the grain." And he did as Joseph had told him.
>
> Genesis 44:1–2

As he had on their first visit to Egypt, Joseph ordered that his brothers' sacks be filled with food and that once again each man's money be tucked into the top of his sack. In addition, Joseph had his own silver cup placed in the top of Benjamin's sack. Then Joseph commanded his steward:

> "Up, follow the men; and when you overtake them, say to them, 'Why have you repaid evil for good? Is not this the one from which

my lord drinks, and which he indeed uses for divination? You have
done wrong in doing this.'"

Genesis 44:4–5

The sons of Jacob were not far from the city when they looked back
and saw the prime minister's steward overtaking them. Once he caught up,
he accused them of stealing from the Egyptian leader. "How could you do
such a deceitful deed, after having been treated so well?"

"We would never do such a thing," the brothers responded. "There's
nothing in these sacks that we weren't given. We came for grain. We took
grain. And if you can find anything else, we will be your slaves. In fact, you
may kill the one who is guilty." That's how certain they were. That's how
positive they were that they were innocent.

They did not hesitate to let the steward examine their sacks of
food, beginning with Reuben, the oldest. But lo and behold, when the
steward got all the way down to the youngest, he found the silver cup
in Benjamin's sack!

To say the brothers were stunned is an understatement. They knew they
hadn't taken the cup. How had it gotten into Benjamin's food sack? As the
enormity of the implications of this circumstantial evidence dawned upon
them, they moved beyond stunned to distraught. In their anguish, "they
tore their clothes" (Gen. 44:13).

They had to return to the city with the steward, of course, where they
were immediately ushered into the prime minister's presence. There, Judah
did the talking.

> So Judah said, "What can we say to my lord? What can we speak?
> And how can we justify ourselves? God has found out the iniquity of
> your servants; behold, we are my lord's slaves, both we and the one in
> whose possession the cup has been found."

Genesis 44:16

This confession from Judah's mouth was amazing. But this was precisely what Joseph had been waiting for; this was why he had given the

final exam. They passed. In fact all the brothers made straight A's on the first part of the test.

In speaking for his brothers, Judah did not attempt to justify himself or the others, nor does he try to pass the blame off onto Benjamin. Unlike before, they didn't turn on Benjamin and reject him as they had Joseph so many years ago. Judah says, in no uncertain terms, they were all guilty.

Given their history, this is an amazing admission. A real change had begun in their attitude. Think about the fact that these words were coming from the mouth and heart of *Judah!*

Joseph wanted to know whether his brothers were able to read the hand of God into daily life, even in things that seemed unfair. Even in misfortune and death. He wanted to see if their vertical scope was clear. And now he heard this confession coming out of Judah's mouth, who laid the guilt on all their shoulders. "Before God we have been found out. We are guilty! Our iniquity has been discovered."

I believe that in his confession Judah was actually going back over twenty years earlier and was referring to those days when they not only hated their brother Joseph but turned against him and sold him into slavery. Had it not been for Reuben, they would have murdered him. This now haunted these men. Judah had begun to realize that God did not overlook an unrepented offense.

THE BARGAIN: BROTHER FOR THE BROTHER

Then Joseph said:

> But he said, "Far be it from me to do this. The man in whose posses-
> sion the cup has been found, he shall be my slave; but as for you, go
> up in peace to your father."
>
> Genesis 44:17

This was Joseph's second part of the final exam. First came the vertical test. Had his brothers gotten to the place where they read the hand of God into their daily life? Yes. They had demonstrated this in their attitude.

Next came the horizontal test. Which would they choose, themselves or Benjamin? Had there been any change in their hearts over the years?

So Joseph said, "I would never punish all of you for one man's crime. The cup has been found in your youngest brother's possession, so he is the one I will punish. He will forfeit his freedom and become my slave. The rest of you, go in peace. You can return to your father."

Following this pronouncement comes a shocking speech which, in the words of Leupold, a reliable German scholar, "stands unexcelled" in the Old Testament.

> Then Judah approached him, and said, "Oh my lord, may your servant please speak a word in my lord's ears, and do not be angry with your servant; for you are equal to Pharaoh. My lord asked his servants, saying, 'Have you a father or a brother?' And we said to my lord, 'We have an old father and a little child of his old age. Now his brother is dead, so he alone is left of his mother, and his father loves him.' Then you said to your servants, 'Bring him down to me, that I may set my eyes on him.' But we said to my lord, 'The lad cannot leave his father, for if he should leave his father, his father would die.' You said to your servants, however, 'Unless your youngest brother comes down with you, you shall not see my face again.' Thus it came about when we went up to your servant my father, we told him the words of my lord. And our father said, 'Go back, buy us a little food.' But we said, 'We cannot go down. If our youngest brother is with us, then we will go down; for we cannot see the man's face unless our youngest brother is with us.' And your servant my father said to us, 'You know that my wife bore me two sons; and the one went out from me, and I said, "Surely he is torn in pieces," and I have not seen him since. And if you take this one also from me, and harm befalls him, you will bring my gray hair down to Sheol in sorrow.' Now, therefore, when I come to your servant my father, and the lad is not with us, since his life is bound up in the lad's life, it will come about when he sees that the lad is not with us, that he will die. Thus your servants will bring the gray hair of your servant our father down to Sheol in sorrow. For your servant became surety for the lad to my father, saying, 'If I do not bring

him back to you, then let me bear the blame before my father forever.'
Now, therefore, please let your servant remain instead of the lad a
slave to my lord, and let the lad go up with his brothers. For how
shall I go up to my father if the lad is not with me, lest I see the evil
that would overtake my father?"

Genesis 44:18–34

Do you realize who is saying this? Again, it is *Judah*. These "unexcelled"
words were coming from the same man who, twenty years earlier, proposed
without remorse, "Here comes that dreamer, Joseph. Let's kill him and say
that a ferocious animal devoured him." Shortly after that cold-blooded pro-
posal, he rationalized, "What will we gain if we kill our brother and cover
up his blood? Let's sell him to the slave traders instead."

Yet here he was, pleading for his youngest brother. Added to that, he
was pleading on behalf of his father.

A few years earlier, Judah could not have cared less what his father
thought, since his father had always shown favoritism to Rachel's sons. In
fact, the violence and cruelty Judah and his brothers perpetrated against
Joseph was an indirect act of cruelty committed against their father.

Now, of all things, this same man is exhibiting a sacrificial attitude. "Take
me instead. But send Benjamin back home. I cannot bear to see this evil
overtake my father." No, it's not the same man; he has changed.

No doubt about it. Judah and his brothers were becoming transformed
men, and Joseph recognized this. Repentance had done its work. They had
passed both parts of the final exam. I believe that this explains why Joseph
decided at this moment to take off his mask of secrecy.

THE DISCLOSURE: IDENTITY OF THE RULER

The following represents one of the greatest moments in the entire Old
Testament—the climax in a story that has held our attention for hours.

Then Joseph could not control himself before all those who stood by
him, and he cried, "Have everyone go out from me." So there was no

man with him when Joseph made himself known to his brothers. And he wept so loudly that the Egyptians heard it, and the household of Pharaoh heard of it. Then Joseph said to his brothers, "I am Joseph! Is my father still alive?" But his brothers could not answer him, for they were dismayed at his presence.

Genesis 45:1–3

Joseph cleared the room of all the Egyptians, all the stewards, servants, and slaves. Only the eleven brothers were left, trembling before him. *What is going to happen now?* they wondered. *What is he going to do to us?*

Suddenly they saw the Egyptian official—a man second only to Pharaoh in importance—break into tears. Not just silent tears, seeping down his cheeks. His outburst was so great that even those outside the room heard it and began telling others in Pharaoh's household about what was happening.

Astonishing words quickly followed the tears.

"I am Joseph!" said the prime minister. "Is my father still alive?"

He broke his silence in both words and language, for he spoke to them for the first time in Hebrew. *"AAA-NEE YO-SAPHE!"* "I am Joseph."

The brothers "were dismayed at his presence." That's putting it mildly! They were stunned. They were speechless. They were terrified! They began to tremble. *Was this some kind of diabolical trap?*

Then Joseph said to his brothers, "Please come closer to me." And they came closer. And he said, "I am your brother Joseph, whom you sold into Egypt."

Genesis 45:4

As they stood there trembling, he said, "Come closer."

The Hebrew verb here, *nah-gash,* refers not just to spatial proximity, but to an intimate closeness. It is a term occasionally used for coming near for the purpose of embracing or kissing someone. It is not the common Hebrew term used for merely coming near or walking up close. The New International Version translates it: "Come close to me." I think this passage may imply that Joseph wanted his brothers to observe his face "up close."

This would provide final evidence that he was, in fact, one of the twelve—not an Egyptian ruler, but their own flesh and blood.

That did it! What they found impossible to believe earlier, they were now forced by that proof to accept what he had said. Their mouths must have dropped open at this moment. He had just revealed the best-kept secret in Canaan. Surely, none of the brothers had ever told anyone what had happened that day, out in the fields near Dothan. How would this man know the truth if he were not their long-lost Joseph? They stared at him, unable to blink, as he reaffirmed, "I am the one you sold into Egypt. *I am Joseph.*"

This is another of those moments that is impossible to describe. Words cannot adequately define the scene or contain it.

Some years ago a television film called *The Promise* told the story of a young man and woman who, almost on the eve of their wedding, were involved in a terrible auto accident in which both were seriously injured and the wife's face was horribly disfigured. While they were recovering in the hospital, in separate rooms, the young man's mother visited her soon-to-be daughter-in-law. This cruel woman had never wanted her son to marry the young woman, and now she saw a way to prevent it. She told the badly injured young woman that she would secretly pay for all the plastic surgery involved to restore her face if the woman promised to disappear and never again have anything to do with her son. Suffering, bewildered, in the midst of her trauma and agony, the disfigured and confused woman made that promise. Shortly thereafter, the mother told her son that his fiancée had been killed in the accident.

Several years later, however, through an unusual chain of events, the young man and woman met. Since he had not changed greatly, she immediately recognized him. She attempted to keep her promise to have nothing to do with him, but gradually, as circumstances brought them together, he began to recognize her. He realized that the woman he had loved so deeply, with a love that still haunted him, was indeed alive. Eventually, they were reunited in a romantic scene of reconciliation.

Years of separation were followed by that beautiful moment of discovery and reconciliation. Anyone who has ever been reunited with a friend or loved one after years of separation knows exactly what this means.

Many years ago, one of our own dear daughters-in-law, Debbie, captured the emotions of such a moment in these words:

> When my eye first caught sight of you I wanted to rush into your arms and embrace my faded memories in the flesh. But fear paralyzed my steps and I stood, desperately clutching the strap of my purse as if it were the only thing keeping me on my feet.
>
> Your hair had grown gray, and as I scanned your face the lines appeared more frequent and deep than I had remembered. Your shoulders stooped a little lower and I wondered if the internal changes had been as great.
>
> At that moment I met your eyes and my anxiety dissolved in their warm blueness. I started to cry at the sight of your smile. You see, it was the same.
>
> I ran into your arms and the tears rolled down my face as these familiar words reached my ears, "I love you."[1]

If you can read Genesis 45 and not be caught up in the same imaginary journey, you have not done justice to Joseph's biography. These few simple, straightforward words, "I am your brother Joseph, whom you sold into Egypt" (v. 4), embody the sea of emotions that washed over these brothers, not the least of which was their lingering guilt. He saw it in their faces. That's why he said what he did next, as he again demonstrated grace in abundance.

THE RESPONSE: GRACE TO THE GUILTY

And now do not be grieved or angry with yourselves, because you sold me here; for God sent me before you to preserve life. For the famine has been in the land these two years, and there are still five years in which there will be neither plowing nor harvesting. And God sent me before you to preserve for you a remnant in the earth, and to keep you

143

alive by a great deliverance. Now, therefore, it was not you who sent me here, but God; and He has made me a father to Pharaoh and lord of all his household and ruler over all the land of Egypt.

Genesis 45:5–8

Humanly speaking, the average individual, when faced with people who have done them such grievous wrong, would likely frown and demand, "Drop to your knees and stay there! You think you know what humiliation is all about. You wait until I'm through with you. I've been waiting all these torturous years for this moment!"

But not Joseph. He was a changed man. He was God's man, which means he was a great man. And so, with the arm of the Lord supporting him, he could look into his brothers' anxious eyes and say, in all sincerity, "Do not be grieved or angry with yourselves because you sold me into slavery. It was not you who sent me here, but God. He sent me before you to preserve life." Allow me a moment to interrupt the flow of events and ask you: Did he operate from the vertical perspective, or what?

"But God!" Those two words change *everything*.

Joseph could never have spoken such words of reassurance if he had not fully forgiven his brothers. You cannot genuinely embrace a person you've not fully forgiven. Joseph did not see his brothers as enemies, because his perspective had been changed. "You didn't send me here," he said. "God sent me here. And He sent me here for a reason—to preserve life."

I love that. In today's terms: "Men, it wasn't you who pulled this off; it was God. It was my sovereign Lord who saw far into the future and saw the needs of this world and chose me to be His personal messenger to solve the famine problem of the future. You thought you were doing evil to me. But I'll tell you, it was God who worked outside your evil intentions to preserve life."

And he says it again, "Now, therefore, it was not you who sent me here, but God." *But God!* Underline that. "God sent me." Joseph was a man who operated his life—continually—with divine perspective.

Years later, Joseph would say this again, when once more his brothers were worried. Though more years had passed they would still be worried about what Joseph might do to them after their father's death. Guilt clings to the side of the boat, clawing for a foothold, long after grace has come on board and begun to steer. That's why Joseph repeated his earlier speech.

> Then his brothers also came and fell down before him and said, "Behold, we are your servants." But Joseph said to them, "Do not be afraid, for am I in God's place? And as for you, you meant evil against me, but God meant it for good in order to bring about this present result, to preserve many people alive."
>
> Genesis 50:18–20

How magnanimous of Joseph! What a magnificent, God-directed attitude!

I don't know what goes on inside your skin, the memories that haunt you, or the pain you live with because of someone's wrongdoing, but I know humanity well enough to know that most of you, at one time or another, have been treated badly by someone. When that happens, your perspective becomes cloudy. You remember the manipulation. You remember the wrong. You remember the unfair treatment. You remember the torturous trauma, the rejection. Evil was done to you. It was *meant* to be evil! This is no time to deny it—the person deliberately hurt you.

Joseph said to his brothers, "You meant it for evil." There was nothing good in their motives—and he said so.

"But God"! Here is where Joseph allowed his theology to eclipse his human emotions and bad memories. An excellent trade-off.

"But God meant it for good."

> "Now, therefore, it was not you who sent me here, but God; and He has made me a father to Pharaoh and lord of all his household and ruler over all the land of Egypt. Hurry and go up to my father, and say to him, 'Thus says your son Joseph, "God has made me lord of all Egypt; come down to me, do not delay."'"
>
> Genesis 45:8–9

Underscore that line: *"God has made me lord of all Egypt."*

"God sent me here. He planned it all. He arranged the events in such a way that nothing was omitted. In the process, brothers, He remade me and gave me this position. Tell my father, I want to offer you a place to live right here near me in Egypt."

> Joseph's words pull back the narrative veil and allow the reader to see what has been going on behind the scenes. It was not the brothers who sent Joseph to Egypt; rather it was God. And God had a purpose for it all. We have seen numerous clues throughout the narrative that this has been the case; but now the central character, the one ultimately responsible for initiating the plots and subplots of the preceding narratives, reveals the divine plans and purpose behind it all. Joseph, who could discern the divine plan in the dreams of Pharaoh, also knew the divine plan in the affairs of his brothers. Through it all he saw God's plan to accomplish a "great deliverance" (v. 7).
>
> In describing God's care over him, Joseph made an allusion to the brothers' initial question regarding his dreams as a young lad. They had said, "Do you intend to reign over us?" (37:8). Now he reminded them that he had been made "ruler of all Egypt" (45:8).[2]

On top of his forgiveness and reassurance, he "made them an offer they couldn't refuse." He urged them to return and bring their father to this land, where they could enjoy relief from their barren existence.

> "'And you shall live in the land of Goshen, and you shall be near me, you and your children and your children's children and your flocks and your herds and all that you have. There I will also provide for you, for there are still five years of famine to come, lest you and your household and all that you have be impoverished.'" And behold, your eyes see, and the eyes of my brother Benjamin see, that it is my mouth which is speaking to you. Now you must tell my father of all my splendor in Egypt, and all that you have seen; and you must hurry and bring my father down here."
>
> Genesis 45:10–13

Joseph said, "Brothers, I have seen a change in your lives. You care about our father and one another and you never did before. You care about Benjamin, more than even your own lives. What a change!"

Attitude is so crucial in the life of the Christian. We can go through the Sunday motions, we can carry out the religious exercises, we can pack a Bible under our arms, and sing the songs from memory, yet we can still hold grudges against the people who have wronged us. In our own way—and it may even be with a little religious manipulation—we'll get back at them. But that is not God's way. Here, He shows us the right way. He gives us the example of Joseph, great man that he was, being supportive, merciful, gracious, generous, and unselfish. He's not through showing how deeply he cares for them. Look at this next scene!

> Then he fell on his brother Benjamin's neck and wept; and Benjamin wept on his neck. And he kissed all his brothers and wept on them, and afterward his brothers talked with him.
>
> Genesis 45:14–15

I would imagine they "talked with him!" They had about twenty-five years' worth of talking to do. And I am confident that every time they went back and started to rehearse their wrongs, Joseph stopped them. "We're not going there. That was then, this is now. God had a plan and it's all worked out for our good and His glory. Let's talk about that."

THE TRUTH: LESSONS FROM THE STORY

The late great preacher, John Henry Jowett, used to say that a minister doesn't deserve an hour to preach a sermon if he can't give it in one sentence. So let me give you this sermon in a sentence:

Greatness is revealed mainly in our attitudes.

If you're under the impression that you are going to be great because of some accomplishment you've achieved but harbor wrong attitudes, you're in for a terrible jolt. Greatness comes in the sweet-spirit attitudes of humility and forgiveness toward your fellowman. Joseph sets before us a magnanimous example. How beautifully forgiving he was, how generous in his mercy.

Thomas Jefferson was correct when he said: "When the heart is right, the feet are swift." Part of the reason we are so sluggish in carrying out the application of God's truth is that our heart isn't right. When that's fixed, we are fleet-footed servants of God.

There are dozens of possibilities for a heart's not being right. The heart may not be right toward that person who never paid back what he owed me. The heart may not be right toward the person who divorced me. The heart may not be right toward a God who took my mate. The heart may not be right toward my now-grown child who took advantage of me. The heart may not be right toward the parent who abused or neglected me or toward the pastor who took unfair advantage of me or toward the teacher who failed me.

It takes God to make the heart right. When I have a wrong attitude, I look at life humanly. When I have a right attitude, I look at life divinely. That's the real beauty of Joseph's life. That's the kernel of truth his life represents. He was great, mainly because of his attitude.

And there are specific lessons that grow out of that single truth. Let me offer at least three for your consideration.

First: *When I'm able, by faith, to see God's plan in my location, my attitude will be right.* God sent me . . . God sent me . . . God sent me. Not until you can relax and see God in your present location will you be useful to Him. A positive theological attitude will do wonders for your geographical latitude.

Second: *When I'm able, by faith, to sense God's hand in my situation, my attitude will be right.* I don't begin the day gritting my teeth, asking, "Why do I have to stay in this situation?" Instead, I believe that He made me the way I am and put me where I am to do what He has planned for me to do. I don't wait for my situation to change before I put my heart into my work. I suggest you give that a try. It's called "blooming where you're planted." There's nothing like an attitude of gratitude to free us up.

Third: *When I'm able, by faith, to accept both location and situation as good, even when there's been evil in the process, my attitude will be right.* When I can say with Joseph, "but God meant it for good," then I become a trophy of grace.

Our Savior is not walking the earth in flesh anymore, so we are called to bear His image to the world around us. By having His attitude in what we do and say, we are saying to the world, "This is the right response to wrong treatment. This is what Jesus would do."

John Newton, who wrote such beloved hymns as "Glorious Things of Thee Are Spoken," "How Sweet the Name of Jesus Sounds," and "Amazing Grace," also wrote another that we seldom hear anymore except in small country churches (which I love to visit). It's really a hymn about having the right attitude.

> How tedious and tasteless the hours
>> when Jesus no longer I see!
> Sweet prospects, sweet birds, and sweet flowers,
> Have all lost their sweetness to me:
> The midsummer sun shines but dim,
>> the fields strive in vain to look gay;
> But when I am happy in Him,
>> December's as pleasant as May.[3]

When your attitude is right, "December's as pleasant as May!" It doesn't matter what time of year it is. It doesn't matter where you live. Your circumstances or conditions don't matter all that much. Your days may be "tedious and tasteless." No problem. It's your attitude that matters the most. You don't have to have clear skies or cool evenings. Because your heart is right, your feet are swift. That's how Joseph made it in the pit as well as on the pinnacle. That's how you're going to make it, whatever your situation.

Is your heart right? Are your feet swift? Are you moving away from people or are you moving toward them? Are you engaged in the business of healing or hurting? Are you adding pressure or relieving it? Are you bringing joy or squelching it? Is your December as pleasant as your May? The only way out of the pit is His way. The only solution to bitterness is His grace.

Too often the fog of the flesh blocks out our ability to see God's plan. Our selfishness pushes away His hand because we want our way. Our location and our situation become irksome assignments, and life becomes a barren, cold, lifeless December.

Joseph shows us that the only way to find happiness in the grind of life is to do so *by faith*. A faith-filled life means all the difference in how we view everything around us. It affects our attitudes toward people, toward location, toward situation, toward circumstances, toward ourselves. Only then do our feet become swift to do what is right. Only then is "December as pleasant as May."

You say you want to be considered great some day? Here's the secret: Walk by faith, trusting God to renew your attitude.

CHAPTER TEN

The Ultimate Family Reunion

Almost every summer when I was growing up, my family vacationed at Carancahua Bay in a small cottage down in South Texas between Palacios and Port Alto. Sometimes those events were more like family reunions. If you have ever been to a family reunion, you'll have no trouble imagining what our reunion was like. What a blast! For almost a week, the Lundys and the Mays and the Fradys and the Swindolls all slept and ate and laughed and sang in that little four-room cottage, named "Bide-a-wee," my granddaddy owned. We're talking wall-to-wall family fun.

We swam and took boat rides, fished, floundered, told jokes, and mainly gorged ourselves on fresh flounder and trout and redfish. Fried oysters and boiled shrimp were also in abundance. We also filled ourselves with biscuits and bacon and eggs in the mornings, along with steaks and ribs cooked on an open-pit barbecue, and homemade pies and cobblers and cakes and always handmade ice cream of various flavors. Everybody in the family had fun—but nobody in the family was thin, needless to say.

Along with us, all sorts of varmints inhabited that old cottage, including mosquitoes, wasps, ticks, scorpions, lizards, and horned toads. Yet none of that seemed to bother anybody, because we were all there as one big family.

We laughed ourselves hoarse as Uncle Jake told his funny stories and as my dad did some of the craziest things anybody could imagine. Because there were so many of us, we slept wherever we could find a spot, packed into that little cottage. I remember laughing myself to sleep under the mosquito netting listening to my dad play one tune after another on his harmonica without using his hands while lying in bed. Someone would yell out the name of a song, and in a split second my father would play it. Then we'd shout out another one and he'd play that one. An old lantern glowed and sputtered in the corner of the cabin and finally burned out as sleep overtook us and snoring replaced singing.

Great memories. As everybody grew up and got older, our reunions got lost in the busyness of getting an education and getting married and rearing new families of kids.

The year we buried my father, I came to the stunning realization that our family reunions were gone for good. Never again would I wade into the shallow water alongside him in the night, with gig in hand, floundering, or pull my end of the seine to draw up a catch of shrimp and mullet. Never again would I sit in the same boat with him and "wait for them to bite" just before dawn. Never again would we harmonize on "Home on the Range" and "You Are My Sunshine." Never again would I hear the whine of his old harmonica as I drifted off to sleep. Precious memories. Vivid, pastel-colored memories on the canvas of my mind. Wonderful memories of the way we were way back then, when life was simple and time seemed to stand still.

To this day, I cannot light a Coleman camping lantern without thinking of my dad who taught me how to do it. Or crank up an outboard motor or clean a mess of fish.

Joseph never saw Carancahua Bay in South Texas, and he never heard "The Way We Were," but I am convinced that in his thirty-plus years there were some scattered pictures of what he had left behind, some of his own pastel-colored memories on the canvas of his mind. Did he, each year on his birthday perhaps, revisit those days in Canaan when he was still with the father who loved him and the brothers with whom he grew up? Did he pause in the busyness of his work and remember when? Did he then sigh and secretly shut the door on those memories, thinking, *I'll never see them again?*

PLANS FOR THE ULTIMATE REUNION

For Joseph, of course, all of that had now changed. His brothers have surprisingly reemerged in Egypt. Through an incredible series of events we have followed with great interest he was brought to the point where he revealed his identity to them. They now knew not only that their brother Joseph was alive, but that he was the prime minister of Egypt! Even more important, they had reconciled their differences and come to terms with all past offenses since he was willing to forgive them for all the wrongs they did to him those many years ago. He told them that God's hand was in it all, and that God's plan was running its perfect course. They had discussed everything that had happened in the intervening years. But things were not yet complete. The desire of Joseph's heart was to see his father and to get all of his family to move to Egypt and to live near him so he could provide for them without reservation and without limitation.

We pick up the story at the point where the news of all these happenings reaches the ears of Pharaoh.

Pharaoh's Acceptance

> Now when the news was heard in Pharaoh's house that Joseph's brothers had come, it pleased Pharaoh and his servants. Then Pharaoh said to Joseph, "Say to your brothers, 'Do this: load your beasts and go to the land of Canaan, and take your father and your households and come to me, and I will give you the best of the land of Egypt and you shall eat the fat of the land.' Now you are ordered, 'Do this: take wagons from the land of Egypt for your little ones and for your wives, and bring your father and come. And do not concern yourselves with your goods, for the best of all the land of Egypt is yours.'"
>
> Genesis 45:16–20

During the seven years of plenty, as we saw earlier, Joseph had built vast storehouses and stocked them with grain from the rich, fertile delta region of the Nile. Thanks to the guidance of God and Joseph's obedience, Egypt had an abundance of food. Now, upon hearing that Joseph's brothers had come to Egypt from Canaan, Pharaoh agreed with his prime minister's plan. His encouraging response gives us a clear indication that everything met with his approval. "Send them back for their households and have them settle here in our land. We will give them the best Egypt has to offer." In fact, Pharaoh takes it a step further: He gives Joseph's brothers wagons to take with them to transport the people and all the possessions of their households. Pharaoh promises "the best of the land of Egypt" will be given to them upon their return. Everyone in the court of Pharaoh applauded Joseph's decision. Imagine the affection and respect these people must have had for Joseph to elicit such a generous response!

So Joseph's brothers did as Pharaoh directed. They must have left enormously encouraged, still trying to believe the grace that was showered upon them. They headed back to Canaan with their pack animals and the transport wagons that had been given to them. A smile was on everyone's face, and for sure, they left a few pounds heavier.

Joseph's Provision

> Then the sons of Israel did so; and Joseph gave them wagons according to the command of Pharaoh, and gave them provisions for the journey. To each of them he gave changes of garments, but to Benjamin he gave three hundred pieces of silver and five changes of garments. And to his father he sent as follows: ten donkeys loaded with the best things of Egypt, and ten female donkeys loaded with grain and bread and sustenance for his father on the journey. So he sent his brothers away, and as they departed, he said to them, "Do not quarrel on the journey."
>
> Genesis 45:21–24

Joseph's brothers not only had plenty to eat on the way, but had also been given new clothing. They had all that they needed—and they once again had it in abundance! These men must have really looked like something when they returned to Canaan, a land drying up under those lingering years of famine.

No doubt they passed starving people and dead or dying animals on their five-or six-day trek to Canaan. And there they were, the backs of their beasts loaded with an abundance of provisions and a line of carts to be used to transport their wives and children and other family members back to Egypt. They did not have to walk; they rode in style, wearing colorful, new, Egyptian-woven garments—like ancient Louis Roth suits and Johnston-Murphy alligator sandals.

Notice, however, the one directive Joseph gave them: "Don't get into an argument on the journey!" He knew those men, didn't he? I can't help but smile at times in these biblical stories when little tidbits like that are inserted. Centuries may come and go, but human nature stays pretty much the same. It's hard to improve on depravity.

Ah, yes. Though guilt had done its work and though there had been changes, Joseph was still wise to his brothers. The original Hebrew term translated "quarrel" here means "to be agitated and perturbed," and it is sometimes used preceding a fight. Joseph knew his brothers. He knew their antagonistic personalities and the things they were prone to do. Practically speaking, I think he probably said this because suddenly they found themselves richer (and fatter!), and that change alone could bring out all kinds of negative reactions.

Not very many men can carry a full cup without its disturbing their equilibrium. Sudden wealth or promotion can be a tottering experience, both for the recipient and those surrounding him or her. Superiority, inferiority, arrogance, and jealousy can easily begin to hold sway. If you question that, check on those who win the lottery. Very few can handle the financial windfall.

Joseph had given his brother Benjamin more than he had given to the other brothers. He gave them all provisions and gave each of them new garments, but he gave Benjamin three hundred shekels of silver and five new garments. No doubt Joseph remembered well what had happened years before when he had been given more than the others, but he had his own reasons for giving Benjamin these items. He didn't want that to result in a fight. "So don't argue about it!" he told his brothers.

I think it is safe to say that we are to trust one another, but we are never to trust one another's nature. That's one of the reasons parents give their children the counsel that they do. Parents understand their children's natures better than their offspring do. It's not a question of trust; it's a matter of knowing the nature within.

Jacob's Response

> Then they went up from Egypt, and came to the land of Canaan to their father Jacob. And they told him, saying, "Joseph is still alive, and indeed he is ruler over all the land of Egypt." But he was stunned, for he did not believe them.
>
> Genesis 45:25–26

Keep in mind here that Jacob knew nothing of what had transpired. The last time he'd seen his sons, he wondered if he would ever see them again. Furthermore, he thought for over twenty-five years that his son Joseph had been dead. Was he in for a shocker! Not only did his sons return from Egypt loaded with supplies and new clothing, but filled with the news that "Joseph is still alive!"

The text says that "He was stunned." Some translations say "His heart fainted." The Hebrew text says, literally, "His heart grew numb." I personally think the aging gentleman was so overwhelmed and shocked by the news that he had a mild coronary.

In his mind and heart, he had buried Joseph years ago. He had given up any hope of ever seeing him again. Now he was told that his long-dead son, his favorite son, was really alive and that he was an important official, ruling as prime minister over the entire land of Egypt. At first, Jacob did not believe them. Not too surprising, right? Then,

> When they told him all the words of Joseph that he had spoken to them, and when he saw the wagons that Joseph had sent to carry him, the spirit of their father Jacob revived. Then Israel

said, "It is enough; my son Joseph is still alive. I will go and see him before I die."

Genesis 45:27–28

At this point, the Scripture says, Jacob's spirit "revived." When his sons reported what Joseph had said and when he saw the evidence of Egyptian generosity before his very eyes, Jacob recognized that his sons were telling him the truth. Joseph was alive! With this realization, Jacob's inner spirit came back to life.

> Only one item is recorded in vv. 25–28 about the brothers' return to Jacob: *Joseph is still living!* Once he hears that, Jacob has little concern about the new clothes, Benjamin's purse, or even the grain carried by the animals. In ch. 37 Jacob did believe his sons when they were lying to him. In ch. 45 Jacob disbelieves his sons when they are being truthful with him. Bad news he accepts; good news he rejects. Jacob's response on hearing that Joseph is alive is parallel to the response of the disciples when they were told that Jesus was alive—shock, unbelief, which eventually turns to uncontrollable joy.
>
> The sons' lengthy conversation with Jacob about Joseph (v. 27a) and the sighting of the wagons (v. 27b) provide prima facie evidence for Jacob that Joseph was indeed alive. No longer did he need to pinch himself to see if he was dreaming (v. 27c). The sons might have been making up the story about Joseph, but the *wagons* supply irrefutable confirmation of the authenticity of their story, more so than the clothing or the three hundred shekels.
>
> Now convinced that Joseph is alive, Jacob resolves to go down to Egypt immediately.[1]

From that moment on, I believe, Jacob had only one thought and objective in mind: seeing his son. He forgot about all the goods lined up outside his tent. He didn't even think about eating, although he was desperately hungry. He thought only about one thing: the ultimate family reunion with his beloved son. The twenty-five-plus years dropped away like a stone in water, as though those years of grief and loss had never been. His son was alive! And Jacob was going to see him before he died.

Yet, Jacob did not jump on his horse and gallop down to Egypt to grab his son. Aside from the fact that his age would have prevented such impulsive action, Jacob had learned some things after all these years. I doubt that the dad slept much that night, or any night until he saw Joseph.

JOURNEY FROM CANAAN TO EGYPT

> So Israel set out with all that he had, and came to Beersheba, and offered sacrifices to the God of his father Isaac. And God spoke to Israel in visions of the night and said, "Jacob, Jacob." And he said, "Here I am." And He said, "I am God, the God of your father; do not be afraid to go down to Egypt, for I will make you a great nation there. I will go down with you to Egypt, and I will also surely bring you up again; and Joseph will close your eyes."
>
> Genesis 46:1–4

Vision from the Lord Himself

Yes, old Jacob had learned some hard lessons about what happened when he did not talk with God and walk with God. Therefore, he wanted to be sure that God was in this. This was a big move for all the family. So although he loaded up his household and began the journey, when he got to Beersheba, close to the southern border of Canaan, he stopped. Before proceeding any farther, he built an altar there, and offered sacrifices to the Lord his God. Thankfully, by now, Jacob had matured into a seasoned and wise old man. He stopped and waited, willing to learn whether the move to Egypt would be accompanied by the presence and blessing of God.

It must have been a great moment when, in the night, he was awakened by the voice of God, calling, "Jacob, Jacob."

"Here I am," he replied quietly.

"I am God, the God of your father, Isaac. Don't be afraid to go down to Egypt, for it is there that I will make you a great nation. I will go down to Egypt with you, and I will also bring you back to this land again. And your son Joseph will be with you when you die."

This is a major moment not only for Jacob and his family, but for all of Israel. This is an early prophetic reference to Israel's great Exodus from Egypt. Go back and read the Lord's words to Jacob once again. Notice the promise, "I will also surely bring you up [to this land] again."

God didn't tell Jacob how long Israel would be in Egypt. Nor did He describe to Jacob how large the nation would become. *We* know that they would be there over four hundred years. *We* know that Israel grew to a nation of somewhere between one and three million people during those years. But all Jacob knew was that God was going with them to Egypt and that He would make Jacob's family a great nation. That's really all the old man needed to hear for the moment. Now he could proceed in peace. But God's final promise of assurance was that He would someday bring all the Hebrews back to Canaan, appropriately called for this reason "the Promised Land."

Making a major move can be one of the most insecure times we ever face in life. Pulling up roots in one place and trying to put them down in another can be not only fearful but depressing. That's why I think it's wise to pause here and understand the value of Jacob's hearing God's voice of approval. I've known people who have taken years to adjust—and some who simply never adjust. For the Christian this is heightened by a sense of wonder over whether God is in the move. And even when we feel assured that God is in it, we can still experience times of uncertainty and discouragement. I'm referring not only to a geographical move but also to a career change or a domestic move from single to married. Big, big changes! The assurance that God is with us during such alterations in lifestyle and adjustment periods is terribly important.

Jacob also illustrates that there is much, much more to consider in a move than more money or greater comfort or ease. Making a move involves much more than accepting an offer for a larger salary or managerial advancement. As children of God, we're to listen to the voice of God and ask, *Is God in this? Does this please Him?* That's why Jacob impresses us here.

"Lord, I have been told that my beloved son is in Egypt and that we have been promised a life of plenty and ease if we go there," says Jacob.

"I know he wants me to come. And I long to see him again. I know that Pharaoh has sent the provisions and the wagons and has promised us the best land in Egypt. But, Lord God of my forefathers, *are You there?* Are You in this?"

Jacob was facing a whole new experience. He was being asked to move from his simple, rural, monotheistic lifestyle in Canaan into the sophisticated and polytheistic lifestyle of Egypt, with all the temptations that would bring. Would he and his descendants lose their distinctiveness?

What we're seeing here is not just a family on the move, but a nation. When Jacob and his family leave Canaan, there will be no Israelites left there, for they *are* Israel! Seventy of them in all, not counting his sons' wives. If they move to Egypt, they will become a nation within a nation. No wonder Jacob said, "God, I want to hear Your voice in this."

Only when he knew God was in it did he make the move. I'm impressed with that. I've said a number of negative things about Jacob in this book, so maybe it's a good time to highlight the other side. He was no spring chicken, this Jacob of Genesis 46. According to Genesis 47:9, he has reached the age of 130. No doubt stooped and wrinkled, snow-white hair and a matching long beard, he was of the age many would consider "too old for a move like that." Says who? Here is why I'm so impressed with Jacob: He wasn't afraid of a challenge, just so long as he knew his Lord was in it. If that meant leaving the familiar country of Canaan and readjusting his life to the new sights and sounds and smells of Goshen, so be it. The risks didn't frighten him nor did the changes he faced.

I love that attitude (here we are again—*attitude!*). Old Jacob "set out with all that he had" and, once he got his Lord's nod of approval at the altar in Beersheba, there was no looking back. Good for you, Jacob—my kinda man!

When the late General Douglas MacArthur celebrated his 75th birthday, he wrote these insightful words:

> In the central place of every heart there is a recording chamber; so long as it receives messages of beauty, hope, cheer, and courage, so long are you young. When the wires are all down and your heart is covered with

the snows of pessimism and the ice of cynicism, then, and then only are you grown old.[2]

Trip to Egypt

> Then Jacob arose from Beersheba; and the sons of Israel carried their father Jacob and their little ones and their wives, in the wagons which Pharaoh had sent to carry him. And they took their livestock and their property, which they had acquired in the land of Canaan, and came to Egypt, Jacob and all his descendants with him.
>
> Genesis 46:5–6

So Jacob and his sons headed out for Egypt, with all their wagonloads of wives and children, sons and daughters, grandsons and granddaughters, and all their possessions and livestock—the works. Shades of *The Grapes of Wrath*. What a caravan!

By the time they arrived in Egypt, these rural, famine-stricken, travel-worn people must have looked like a vagabond bunch, loaded down with their crying babies and personal belongings and cattle. Nevertheless, they entered the great land of the Pharaohs.

Scholars have estimated that Jacob moved to Egypt about 1876 B.C., which falls within the era known as the Middle Kingdom and the Twelfth Dynasty. According to historians, this was a period of great power and stability in Egypt. Military campaigns and mining expeditions to outlying provinces and neighboring countries made Egypt a dominant, international, almost imperial, power. The development of its economy, as well as achievements in education, sculpture, architecture, and literature, made this a classic period. Their writings became the authoritative texts of later centuries.

This, then, was the Egypt into which Jacob and his descendants made their way.

One can only imagine their awe as they marched into a world of such efficiency, beauty, and cultural magnificence. Beautiful cities. Prosperous people. And one can only imagine what the Egyptians must have thought when they saw what appeared to be "a bunch of hillbillies" coming through the gates. They could laugh if they wished, but Jehovah God was with them, which made them invincible.

REUNION WITH JOSEPH

> Now he sent Judah before him to Joseph, to point out the way before
> him to Goshen; and they came into the land of Goshen.
>
> Genesis 46:28

Joseph had been waiting for this glorious day. He had been imagining this reunion for over twenty-five years. Did he pace his chamber at night, wondering if his brothers would return, agonizing over whether his father would still be alive when they got back to Canaan, and if he were, would the stubborn old man believe them and return with them?

Arrival at Goshen

Finally the day came when his scouts sent word that the caravan he'd been waiting for could be seen on the horizon. (You know Joseph had scouts out there. You know this man had *everything* prepared.)

Judah traveled on ahead to get directions. But Joseph didn't just give or send directions. He jumped into his own chariot and went out to meet his father.

Father-Son Encounter

And then comes that wonderful moment—another scene where words fail.

> And Joseph prepared his chariot and went up to Goshen to meet his
> father Israel; as soon as he appeared before him, he fell on his neck
> and wept on his neck a long time.
>
> Genesis 46:29

Pause, and let the wonder sink in.

I love the terse yet descriptive manner in which the historian, Alfred Edersheim, portrays this intimate reunion:

On his journey Jacob sent Judah in advance, to inform Joseph of his arrival. He hastened to receive his father in the border-land of Goshen. Their meeting, after so long a parting, was most affectionate and touching. The Hebrew expression, rendered in our Authorized Version: "Joseph . . . presented himself unto him," implies extraordinary splendour of appearance. But when in the presence of his Hebrew father, the great Egyptian lord was once more only the lad Joseph.[3]

Think of what it must have been like. After more than two decades, Jacob once more held the son that he had given up for dead. After all he had been through, Joseph embraced his aging father—the man he had missed so much, the one he feared he would never see again. He could feel the bones across his back as he held the old man in his arms. How long it had been! How much he had missed him! There the two men stood, staring into each other's eyes. Weeping one moment, laughing the next. *What a grand family reunion.*

This reminds me of an article I read in the *Fullerton News Tribune* some years back, which told the story of the meeting of twins who had been separated at birth. They knew they were adopted, but they had no idea who their biological parents were. Through the help of a third party, they were brought together. But when their pictures appeared in the paper, telling about their adult reunion, a third identical person appeared. They were triplets! As excited and dumbfounded as those three men must have been, I suggest that this ultimate family reunion was even greater. Jacob said the only fitting thing as soon as he could control himself: "Now let me die, since I have seen your face, that you are still alive" (Genesis 46:30).

LOOKING BACK, LOOKING FORWARD

In thinking of this glorious family reunion, my mind turns to other reunions that brought forth tears of ecstasy. Travel back with me to a few select historical settings.

In Ezra and Nehemiah we read of a *national reunion.* The nation (Judah) had been in captivity for over seventy years. Finally, the king said, "You can go back to your land." Jerusalem had been destroyed. Hardly a stone was left standing. So the people began to rebuild the wall as well as the place of worship, and they gathered in the city square to hear the Word of God read for the first time in decades.

They had been in captivity for seventy years. What nationalistic zeal and pride must have surged through those Jewish veins as they stood once more in their homeland and heard Ezra begin to read aloud the Word of their God. The result is recorded for us in Nehemiah's journal:

> Then Nehemiah, who was the governor, and Ezra the priest and scribe, and the Levites who taught the people said to all the people, "This day is holy to the LORD your God; do not mourn or weep." For all the people were weeping when they heard the words of the law. Then he said to them, "Go, eat of the fat, drink of the sweet, and send portions to him who has nothing prepared; for this day is holy to our Lord. Do not be grieved, for the joy of the LORD is your strength." So the Levites calmed all the people, saying, "Be still, for the day is holy; do not be grieved." And all the people went away to eat, to drink, to send portions and to celebrate a great festival, because they understood the words which had been made known to them.
>
> Nehemiah 8:9–12

When they heard the Word of God in their own ears for the first time after all those years—some of them for *the first time ever*—they lifted up their hands in praise and they wept aloud.

Think of it. These people had been like POWs—prisoners of war—in captivity not for a few years, but for decades. Sometimes, as had happened with this great nation, familiarity with the blessings of God's Word breeds contemptuous and disobedient spirits. As a result, they had suffered from feelings of distance from God during their rigors of captivity. Then suddenly they were freed, able to return to their beloved homeland. The oldest ones, older and grayer. The youngest, who had spent their entire lives in captivity, entered a whole new experience. Once again they could gather together in a place of worship and hear the Word of the Lord. And with their arms outstretched to the heavens, they could do nothing but cry out with tears of ecstasy. This national reunion must have been something to behold.

Another reunion of an altogether different kind is mentioned in the New Testament. I'm thinking of that time when Jesus told the story of the prodigal son. In doing so He spoke of *a personal reunion.*

The prodigal son said, "I have the right to my inheritance and my freedom, father. Give it to me so I can get on with my own life."

His father, without arguing, turned over the money, and the boy set off on his own destructive path. When he had fallen into the pit of his own making, eating slop with the hogs, he finally came to his senses and headed for home.

That's always the way it is when we take a trip down Carnal Lane. We always come to a dead end. Everything we've been looking for is really back home with God.

As he came over the horizon, I can only imagine that wasted son, who already had his speech ready, thinking, *I'm going to apologize and tell my father I repent and beg for his forgiveness. I will beg him to take me back.*

Before he could get the words out of his mouth, however, his father ran to meet him, embraced him, and kissed him repeatedly. What a reunion!

Author David Redding describes his own feelings about a time in his earlier years when "coming home" meant so much to him.

I remember going home from the Navy for the first time during World War II. Home was so far out in the country that when we went hunting we had to go toward town. We had moved there for my father's health when I was just 13. We raised cattle and horses.

I started a little flock of Shropshire sheep, the kind that are completely covered by wool except for a black nose and the tips of black legs. My father helped them have their twins at lambing time, and I could tell each one of the flock apart at a distance with no trouble. I had a beautiful ram. Next door was a poor man who had a beautiful dog and a small flock of sheep he wanted to improve with my ram. He asked me if he could borrow the ram; in return he would let me have the choice of the litter from his prize dog.

That is how I got Teddy, a big, black Scottish shepherd. Teddy was my dog, and he would do anything for me. He waited for me to come home from school. He slept beside me, and when I whistled he ran to me even if he were eating. At night no one could get within a half mile without Teddy's permission. During those long summers in the fields I would only see the family at night, but Teddy was with me all the time. And so when I went away to war, I didn't know how to leave him. How do you explain to someone who loves you that you are leaving him and will not be chasing woodchucks with him tomorrow like always?

So, coming home that first time from the Navy was something I can scarcely describe. The last bus stop was fourteen miles from the farm. I got off there that night at about eleven o'clock and walked the rest of the way home. It was two or three in the morning before I was within a half mile of the house. It was pitch dark, but I knew every step of the way. Suddenly Teddy heard me and began his warning bark. Then I whistled only once. The barking stopped. There was a yelp of recognition, and I knew that a big black form was hurtling toward me in the darkness. Almost immediately he was there in my arms. To this day that is the best way I can explain what I mean by coming home.

What comes home to me now is the eloquence with which that unforgettable memory speaks to me of my God. If my dog, without any explanation, would love me and take me back after all that time, wouldn't my God?[4]

These stories lead us to one other type of reunion noted in Scripture—*the final, ultimate family reunion* that is the hope of every child of God. We read of it in Paul's writings to the Thessalonians.

But we do not want you to be uninformed, brethren, about those who are asleep, that you may not grieve, as do the rest who have no hope. For if we believe that Jesus died and rose again, even so God will bring with Him those who have fallen asleep in Jesus. For this we say to you by the word of the Lord, that we who are alive, and remain until the coming of the Lord, shall not precede those who have fallen asleep. For the Lord Himself will descend from heaven with a shout, with the voice of the archangel, and with the trumpet of God; and the dead in Christ shall rise first. Then we who are alive and remain shall be caught up together with them in the clouds to meet the Lord in the air, and thus we shall always be with the Lord. Therefore comfort one another with these words.

1 Thessalonians 4:13–18

What comfort this brings! What a moment that will be! When all God's people join together in the presence of the living Christ. There are no words sufficient to describe it. Song writers seem to do it best. Hymn writer James M. Black, put it this way many years ago:

> When the trumpet of the Lord shall sound and time shall be no more
> And the morning breaks eternal, bright and fair—
> When the saved of earth shall gather over on the other shore
> And the roll is called up yonder, I'll be there!
>
> On that bright and cloudless morning when the dead in Christ shall rise
> And the glory of His resurrection share—
> When His chosen ones shall gather to their home beyond the skies
> And the roll is called up yonder, I'll be there![5]

On that day, we'll all hear the blast of a trumpet. I know some who expect to hear the melodious strings of a harp. Not me. I expect to hear the lonely whine of a harmonica—because my dad is there in glory, awaiting my arrival. And on that "great gettin'-up morning" our entire family will be reunited forever in the presence of the Lord.

The reality is, though, that no matter how precious your memories, it does not matter the way you were. What matters is the way you are. No amount of solid family ties will fit you for heaven. Only through Christ will you be included in His family roll call.

We can be thankful for the recording chamber of our memories that keeps us young. But what we really need at this important moment is the deep assurance that we are His. Only then can we look forward in hope to that ultimate and final family reunion.

CHAPTER ELEVEN

On-the-Job Integrity

A young man was overheard making a phone call at a pay phone. After the fellow dropped in his coins and punched in the number, the eavesdropper heard the following comments.

"Sir, could you use an honest, hard-working, capable employee?" the young man asked. "No? . . . Oh, you already have one? Well, thanks anyway," he said, and hung up. As he turned away, he was smiling and began to whistle his way back to his car.

"Young man, I couldn't help overhearing you," said the listener. "Am I right in thinking that you just got turned down for a job?"

"Yep," grinned the fellow.

"So what have you got to smile and be so happy about?"

"Because *I am* the honest, hard-working, capable employee they already have. I was just checking up on my job."

If you disguised your voice over the phone and asked your manager or your boss the same question, what answer would you get? Would he or she say, "I'm sorry. That job is already filled with just the right person." Or would you hear: "Sure, we need the kind of person you're describing. Could you come in for an interview?"

It amazes me how little is said from pulpits or by Christian authors about our occupations. How little we hear about the importance of our working lives, yet that is what consumes a major portion of our energy each week. I'm of the opinion that we need to give more attention to our work, the place where we are employed, the place where we spend most of our time and where we earn our living. Why?

First, *work offers a revealing display of character.* It is not our behavior on Sunday morning that demonstrates the depth of our Christian faith to the world. It's the way we behave at our work, on the job. You ask a person who works alongside you or under you or over you or on the same team about your Christianity and that person will not talk about your life on Sunday. That person will talk about what you are like to work with or to work for, day after day after day, all week long.

Your actions and attitude on the job display your character. Any negative traits quickly come to the forefront: sloth, deception, dishonesty, anger, greed, discord, gossip, pettiness, lack of confidentiality, disloyalty, impatience—you name it. On the bright side, of course, positive traits are also on display: ambition, punctuality, honesty, a good sense of humor, harmony, congeniality, commitment, teamwork, enthusiasm, willingness to serve others, loyalty, diligence, encouragement, support, generosity—to name a few.

Someone said, "Business is a lot like the game of tennis. Those who don't serve well end up losing." This is certainly true when it comes to our work.

Second, *the job is a demanding arena of pressure.* Many of you know that all too well, because right now you are living with the kind of pressure that taps and saps, drains your energy, and demands your best efforts.

There is the pressure of the workload. As you look at your desk, buried beneath mounds of paper, unmet deadlines, unanswered E-mail, you often feel that you will never, ever catch up. The stack is so high, your in-box is beginning to resemble the Leaning Tower of Pisa.

There is the pressure of working with people. In one way or another, we all work with people. (Even the sleepy Maytag repairman occasionally has to deal with customers!)

There's pressure from office pettiness or profanity or gossip. There's the pressure of being the one who has to put out the fires, even those little brush fires that must be contained before they grow into forest fires.

Again, one sage has said, "You can tell a company by the personnel it keeps." And in that regard, some of you are under pressure because your company is downsizing or reorganizing, and you're not sure you'll have your job much longer. Or perhaps you have a boss who is so unreasonable that you can't take the pressure anymore and know you must leave.

I read of a large ad agency in New York City whose quick-tempered boss fires about four employees a day. Anybody who lasts a full year is secretly given a prize by astounded colleagues. One of the vice presidents of the agency, recalling the first day he started working there, said with a sigh, "I didn't mind too much that my name was printed on the door with chalk, but I did think that the wet sponge hanging on the doorknob was highly unethical!"

No doubt about it, the workplace is a demanding arena of pressure that reveals character.

Third, *work is an exacting test of efficiency.* Are we well organized? Are we decisive? Can we make tough decisions? Can we think creatively? Do we meet our deadlines? Maintain our budgets? Accomplish our goals? Do we finish tasks delegated to us? Do we follow through with sufficient follow up? Are we willing to be accountable? How perceptive are we? Do we spot flaws and weaknesses and potential problems before they happen? With tongue in cheek, a friend said the other day, "Everybody ought to be paid what he is worth, no matter how big a cut he might have to take."

This is a good time to ask a theological question: Is God not sovereign over all realms, including the realm of our employment? Since when did character take a vacation from business? And whoever said that our faithfulness at church is more important than our faithfulness at work? Somehow I've never been able to understand how followers of Christ could separate life into separate segments, calling one secular and the other sacred.

When it comes to character on the job, we can learn some valuable lessons from Joseph.

A SPECIFIC MODEL WORTH EMULATING: JOSEPH

The Egyptian prime minister is a fine example to follow. As we'll soon see, he didn't compartmentalize his life into many independent, disconnected, fragmented pieces. Rather, he lived an integrated life of wholesome integrity.

As the prime minister, he was second in authority only to Pharaoh. Not only was he the top government employee, he held the job at a critical time of transition. There had been plenty; now there was a famine. This famine had been in the land for the past two years, and thanks to the wisdom God had given him, Joseph knew that the dire situation would continue for five more years.

A seven-year famine! Think of the insecurity, the fear, the panic, such an ordeal would create. Think of the responsibility, the weight of it. Joseph felt all of that, on top of which he now had the added responsibility of his family. And this wasn't just a single family unit—mother, father, and a couple of kids. This was some seventy people—a small nation! And they were Hebrews from Canaan trying to set up housekeeping in a whole new environment in Goshen of Egypt.

How was Joseph going to handle all of this responsibility? What did he do to accomplish all his tasks without compromising his integrity? Were there some secrets we can uncover as we examine his workload?

First, *Joseph planned ahead with wise objectivity.*

> And Joseph said to his brothers and to his father's household, "I will go up and tell Pharaoh, and will say to him, 'My brothers and my father's household, who were in the land of Canaan, have come to me; and the men are shepherds, for they have been keepers of livestock; and they have brought their flocks and their herds and all that they have.' And it shall come about when Pharaoh calls you and says, 'What is your occupation?' that you shall say, 'Your servants have been keepers of livestock from our youth even until now, both we and our fathers,' that you may live in the land of Goshen; for every shepherd is loathsome to the Egyptians."
>
> Genesis 46:31–34

Joseph did his homework. He did not simply look across the landscape, find the best spot, and then tell his father and brothers, "Look, you guys can settle over there. I'll handle it with Pharaoh." No, Joseph was willingly accountable to Pharaoh. He refused to presume on his superior. Furthermore, he never took unfair advantage by reminding Pharaoh that he, Joseph, was the one who, years ago, had warned of the coming famine.

Joseph efficiently thought through a plan of operation that would get his family settled. He rehearsed the plan with those who were involved and then, as we will see in a moment, presented the plans to his boss for final approval. Joseph never assumed that he could just go ahead with his plans, despite his high level of authority and responsibility. He always deferred to his employer.

One complaint that I often hear leveled against Christian employees who work for Christian employers is presumption—the expectation of special treatment because they're members of the same spiritual family. They expect certain privileges, higher salary or vacation perks or other benefits, not because they have earned or deserve them, but simply because they are members of the same church or serve the same Lord. We see none of that happening with Joseph.

Joseph knew how the Egyptians thought and reacted. He had not only worked with Pharaoh but had thoroughly studied and observed the man and his people. That explains why he warned his brothers, "Look, shepherds are loathsome to these people. You're not in Canaan anymore, you're in Egypt. And when you're in Egypt, you have to think like an Egyptian. So I want you to tell Pharaoh that you are keepers of livestock." This was the truth. He wasn't asking them to lie, but to avoid using a word or concept—*shepherd*—that was repugnant to Pharaoh and his people.

Frank Goble, in his outstanding book, *Excellence in Leadership*, talks about this kind of objectivity when he stated: "Excellent leaders have the ability to see things realistically. They are not easily deceived by others, nor do they practice self-deception."[1]

Arthur Maslow added,

> One of the most striking superiorities reported of self-actualizing people
> is their exceptional perceptiveness. They can perceive truth and reality

173

far more efficiently than the average run of people. . . . Our subjects see human nature as it *is* and not as they would prefer it to be. . . . The first form in which this capacity was noticed was as an unusual ability to detect the spurious, the fake, and the dishonest in personality, and in general to judge people correctly and efficiently.[2]

The person who reaches the top of his or her organization, the person who is promoted to a leadership position, is usually a person who has this objective perceptiveness, this ability to see the truth rather than operating on the basis of what one wishes were true. This was certainly the way Joseph operated with Pharaoh, the Egyptians, and even his own family.

Second, *Joseph submitted to authority with loyal accountability.*

> Then Joseph went in and told Pharaoh, and said, "My father and my brothers and their flocks and their herds and all that they have, have come out of the land of Canaan; and behold, they are in the land of Goshen." And he took five men from among his brothers, and presented them to Pharaoh. . . . Then Joseph brought his father Jacob and presented him to Pharaoh; and Jacob blessed Pharaoh. . . . So Joseph settled his father and his brothers, and gave them a possession in the land of Egypt, in the best of the land, in the land of Rameses, as Pharaoh had ordered.
>
> 47:1–2, 7, 11

As soon as Joseph had his family settled in one place, he went to Pharaoh and told him that his family had reached Egypt. First he took five of his brothers, as family representatives, and presented them to Pharaoh; then Joseph introduced his father to Pharaoh.

Pharaoh talked with Joseph's brothers about their future in Egypt and told them that the land was at their disposal. He also had quite a conversation with Jacob, during which he asked the patriarch's age and learned about some of the old man's life experiences.

Joseph settled his family in the choicest part of the land of Egypt, in an area located in the fertile Nile Delta, as Pharaoh had ordered him to do.

This area was called the land of Goshen or the region of Zoan. It is also called "the district of Rameses," which, probably refers to the great Egyptian pharaoh Rameses II, who reigned several centuries later.

Do you serve under someone else's authority? Obviously, most of us do. How's your spirit, your attitude, toward that person to whom you answer? Having the right attitude or spirit can be especially tough if the person to whom you answer is a difficult individual or an incompetent leader or one whose weaknesses you know all too well. This is not only a test of your loyalty, but a test of your Christian maturity.

One interesting sidelight here is the fact that during their conversation with Pharaoh, Joseph's brothers failed to do as he had instructed them.

> Then Pharaoh said to his brothers, "What is your occupation?" So they said to Pharaoh, "Your servants are shepherds, both we and our fathers."
>
> Genesis 47:3

Remember, he had told them to say they were keepers of livestock, because the Egyptians did not hold shepherds in high esteem. Yet when Pharaoh asks their occupation, they tell him that they are shepherds. Joseph doesn't intervene, however; he stands back, folds his arms, and lets them say what they wish. Joseph was a strong, efficient, capable leader, but he was also flexible enough to give his followers responsibility and choices.

His brothers also let Pharaoh know that they weren't asking to live *forever* in the land of Egypt. They asked if they could "sojourn in the land," or to put it another way, they asked if they could stay awhile in the land, because the famine in Canaan had temporarily destroyed their pasture land.

A leader must be wise and flexible, willing to give here and there, willing to delegate, willing to listen to alternative plans and ideas of those alongside. Everything doesn't have to be *your* way. You are responsible for the oversight and the direction, but that does not mean you have the right to squelch every bit of the innovation. Many a church or organization has lost good people exactly because of this kind of inflexibility.

As an employee, Joseph was loyal, accountable, wise, objective, and efficient. As a leader, he was efficient, wise, objective, and flexible. There was also a quiet and secure calmness in his leadership that is beautiful to watch.

Which brings us to a third characteristic of Joseph. *He arranged for survival with personal integrity.* We're back to this quality of integrity again. It surfaces over and over in the man's life and leadership. In this case, notice how thoroughly he was trusted.

> Now there was no food in all the land, because the famine was very severe, so that the land of Egypt and the land of Canaan languished because of the famine. And Joseph gathered all the money that was found in the land of Egypt and in the land of Canaan for the grain which they bought, and Joseph brought the money into Pharaoh's house. And when the money was all spent in the land of Egypt and in the land of Canaan, all the Egyptians came to Joseph and said, "Give us food, for why should we die in your presence? For our money is gone."
>
> Genesis 47:13–15

As the years of famine progressed, everyday life as they had once enjoyed it deteriorated, not unlike the Great Depression years in America, and the people began to panic. Their very survival was at stake. At that point, Joseph was given enormous power. He held their lives, their future, in the palm of his hand. After all, Joseph not only built the granaries, he carried the keys.

What a perfect opportunity for a leader to rip off the public! To stash away some of the money. To give food only to his family or a few of his favorites. With the complete trust that Pharaoh put in him, Joseph wasn't about to be second-guessed.

After all, Joseph had to live with Joseph. Even more importantly, Joseph had to face his God. So the distribution was done decently and in order. All the money went into the proper account. There was no payola, no kickback. He never set up some kind of offshore account; there was no secret slush fund. Joseph operated with absolute integrity and in doing so guaranteed the survival of the Egyptians, the Canaanites, the Hebrews, and other countries. When he had worked for Potiphar, many years earlier, he evidenced the same trustworthiness as he does now. Over two decades have passed, his roles have changed dramatically, but his integrity remained intact.

Why was Joseph like this? A hint is given back in Genesis 41:33 when Joseph, after interpreting Pharaoh's dreams as predicting seven years of abundance and seven years of famine, warned: "And now let Pharaoh look for a man discerning and wise, and set him over the land of Egypt." God had been preparing Joseph for the very position he predicted would be needed for a long time.

The word *discerning* in that statement Joseph made means to have shrewd insight into a situation and its needs. That's a quality a leader must have. It amounts to a sixth sense of anticipation.

A leader must also be *wise*. That word, in the Hebrew, is most often used with constructive activity attached to it. A wise leader is a builder, not a destroyer. "Pharaoh, you need someone who will not split the land apart. You'll have enough trouble with the famine. You need to have a man who can rally the people together and then keep them together."

Tough task, keeping people together when they're starving. How can that be done? Well, among other things, you believe in human dignity. You don't take advantage of people who are at your mercy.

Several years ago I met with a young man who had just come out of an abusive church situation with cultlike tendencies where the leadership modeled intimidation and humiliation to "keep people in line" (his words). I can still remember his telling me, "The thing that was destroyed in me while I was in that situation was my personal dignity. There was no sense of individual worth or significance or freedom. No grace. People were not allowed to think independently or question decisions or take another position on issues without being called into question and humiliated. The pastor and his associates expected respect, but they, themselves, respected no one."

The people came to Joseph with their hands empty and open, and he responded by upholding their dignity and treating them with respect. And keep in mind, he had everything, but they had nothing. "Our money is gone! Our food is gone!" They were completely at Joseph's mercy.

> Then Joseph said, "Give up your livestock, and I will give you food
> for your livestock, since your money is gone." So they brought their
> livestock to Joseph, and Joseph gave them food in exchange for the
> horses and the flocks and the herds and the donkeys; and he fed them
> with food in exchange for all their livestock that year.
>
> Genesis 47:16–17

He didn't shrug his shoulders and give them a handout. He didn't put
them on welfare. Instead, he told them to bring him what they had—their
livestock—and in exchange he would give them food. This method of
exchange went on for an entire year. That's one of the major reasons they
survived the famine.

> And when that year was ended, they came to him the next year and
> said to him, "We will not hide from my lord that our money is all
> spent, and the cattle are my lord's. There is nothing left for my lord
> except our bodies and our lands. "Why should we die before your eyes,
> both we and our land? Buy us and our land for food, and we and our
> land will be slaves to Pharaoh. So give us seed, that we may live and
> not die, and that the land may not be desolate."
>
> So Joseph bought all the land of Egypt for Pharaoh, for every
> Egyptian sold his field, because the famine was severe upon them.
> Thus the land became Pharaoh's. And as for the people, he removed
> them to the cities from one end of Egypt's border to the other. Only
> the land of the priests he did not buy, for the priests had an allotment
> from Pharaoh, and they lived off the allotment which Pharaoh gave
> them. Therefore, they did not sell their land. Then Joseph said to the
> people, "Behold, I have today bought you and your land for Pharaoh;
> now, here is seed for you, and you may sow the land. And at the harvest
> you shall give a fifth to Pharaoh, and four-fifths shall be your own for
> seed of the field and for your food and for those of your households
> and as food for your little ones." So they said, "You have saved our
> lives! Let us find favor in the sight of my lord, and we will be Pharaoh's
> slaves." And Joseph made it a statute concerning the land of Egypt

valid to this day, that Pharaoh should have the fifth; only the land of
the priests did not become Pharaoh's.

Genesis 47:18–26

A year later, with the famine still going strong, all of their livestock were
gone, and they were back on their knees with their hands empty and open,
saying, "Help us, Joseph. What do we do now? Buy our land for food. *Buy
us*—we will serve Pharaoh. Only help us get through these awful years." In
their desperation, they put themselves entirely at Joseph's mercy.

What is striking is that Joseph did not abuse that power—not once!
God had raised him up from slavery and he never forgot how marvelous a
deliverance that was. To whom much has been given, much is required.

Arthur Gordon, writing for a national periodical, says this about the
importance of personal integrity:

> Year after year businessmen study college records, screen applicants, and
> offer special inducement to proven people. What are they after, really?
> Brains? Energy? Know-how? These things are desirable, sure. But they
> will carry a person only so far. If he is to move to the top and be entrusted
> with command decisions, there must be a plus factor, something that
> takes mere ability and doubles or trebles its effectiveness. To describe
> this magic characteristic there is only one word: integrity.[3]

Integrity keeps your eyes on your own paper during the test. Integrity
makes you record and submit only true figures on your expense account.
Integrity keeps your personal life pure and straight, regardless of the benefits
and personal perks that might come your way through compromise.

A successful executive, a member of one of my former churches, once
told me that many years ago, when he was beginning to make his way to
the top of his field, a large company contacted him and promised him the
moon. They interviewed him, wined and dined him, and offered him an
unbelievable salary. That evening when he returned to his hotel room, he
walked in and found a woman waiting for him. She had been hired and
provided by his prospective employers. He sent her away, left the hotel,

took the last flight out that same night. The very next day he wrote to the company, saying, "Forget it. If that's the way you do business, you don't want me."

Max DePree, outstanding Christian businessman, maintains that "Integrity in all things precedes all else. The open demonstration of integrity is essential."

Make no mistake, integrity is tough stuff. Integrity does not take the easy way, make the easy choices, or choose the "pleasures for a season" path. Above all, integrity is what you are when there isn't anyone around to check up on you; it's best demonstrated when nobody's watching.

Since I'm referring to integrity so often in this book, it is time we examine its definition more carefully. My friend, Warren Wiersbe, does a masterful job of that in his book, *The Integrity Crisis:*

> What is *integrity?* The *Oxford English Dictionary* says that the word comes from the Latin *integritas*, which means "wholeness," "entireness," "completeness." The root word is *integer*, which means "untouched," "intact," "entire." Integrity is to personal or corporate character what health is to the body or 20/20 vision is to the eyes. A person with integrity is not divided (that's *duplicity*) or merely pretending (that's *hypocrisy*). He or she is "whole"; life is "put together," and things are working together harmoniously. People with integrity have nothing to hide and nothing to fear. Their lives are open books. They are integers.[4]

Later, Wiersbe points out three salient characteristics of someone with integrity:

> Jesus made it clear that integrity involves the whole of the inner person: the heart, the mind, and the will. The person with integrity has a *single heart*. He doesn't try to love God and the world at the same time. . . . The person with integrity also has a *single mind*, a single outlook ("eye") that keeps life going in the right direction. After all, outlook helps to determine outcome; "a double-minded man [is] unstable in all his ways" (James 1:8). . . . Jesus also said that the person with integrity has a *single*

will; he seeks to serve but one master. Peter T. Forsythe was right when he said, "The first duty of every soul is to find not its freedom but its Master." Once you find your Master, Jesus Christ, you will find your freedom; "therefore if the Son makes you free, you shall be free indeed" (John 8:36). Nobody can successfully serve two masters. To attempt to do so is to become a fractional person, and a fractional person doesn't have integrity. He is someone with a divided heart, a divided mind, and a divided will.[5]

With a single heart, mind, and will Joseph dealt fairly and honestly with all who trusted him with their money. When they held up their hands and passionately declared, "We'll do anything!" he remained fair and compassionate.

Integrity has several components, as we saw in Warren Wiersbe's comments. And those components lead to obvious and beneficial by-products. Among the most important is truthfulness—absolute and uncompromising honesty. Sometimes I think we're better at that element when we're younger. As innocent, naive little children, truth telling seems to flow more easily. Before we learn to lie, we say what is, regardless.

Jerry White, in his book, *Honesty, Morality and Conscience*, tells this story:

> A salesman knocked on the door of a run-down and obviously poor home. The mother in the home told her little boy to tell the salesman she could not come to the door because she was in the bathtub. The little boy went to the door and said, "We ain't got no bathtub, but Mom told me to tell you she's in it."[6]

The honesty of a child! As we get older, however, it's not uncommon to watch folks slide down the slippery slope of dishonesty. We can become increasingly proficient in compromise.

In the aftermath of the Watergate scandal, many keen-thinking people analyzed it in three words: compromise of integrity. The late President Nixon and those surrounding him ultimately revealed an astonishing lack of integrity. Duplicity and hypocrisy abounded. In reading the transcripts of the hours of tape recordings from the discussions in the Oval Office, one can clearly trace the fall. First came the erosion of character, next the threat, then the temptation, the breakdown, the compromise, and finally the rationalization. When there is a breakdown of integrity, we are swamped in the backwash of lies and cover-up. But never forget—at the heart of the problem was an absence of character in our national leader.

Joseph had character. That's why he refused to compromise his integrity. He planned ahead with wise objectivity. He submitted to authority with loyal accountability. He arranged for survival with personal integrity. Finally, *he accepted the challenge with innovative creativity.*

The famine-stricken people had given up everything they had in exchange for food—their livestock, their land, and even themselves. What was Joseph to do? The account in Genesis 47 gives us the answer.

> So Joseph bought all the land of Egypt for Pharaoh, for every Egyptian sold his field, because the famine was severe upon them. Thus the land became Pharaoh's. And as for the people, he removed them to the cities from one end of Egypt's border to the other. Only the land of the priests he did not buy, for the priests had an allotment from Pharaoh, and they lived off the allotment which Pharaoh gave them. Therefore, they did not sell their land. Then Joseph said to the people, "Behold, I have today bought you and your land for Pharaoh; now, here is seed for you, and you may sow the land. And at the harvest you shall give a fifth to Pharaoh, and four-fifths shall be your own for seed of the field and for your food and for those of your households and as food for your little ones." So they said, "You have saved our lives! Let us find favor in the sight of my lord, and we will be Pharaoh's slaves." And Joseph made it a statute concerning the land of Egypt valid to this day, that Pharaoh should have the fifth; only the land of the priests did not become Pharaoh's.
>
> Genesis 47:20–26

Joseph had an innovative plan, something that had never been done before. "In order for the land to produce, we must spread out over this land," he said. Prior to this they had been settled in only a few well-populated regions. Those places represented their homes, their work, their farms, their neighborhoods. They were asked to relinquish all that. That took some selling—an awful lot of convincing. But Joseph managed it, and he spread the people out across the land of Egypt, "from one end of Egypt's border to another."

"You have seed. You can plant," Joseph said. "And if you do that, some-day you will be able to harvest. You will once again have your own income. You'll be able to make it for yourself." He made only one stipulation: "At harvest you shall give a fifth to Pharaoh. The rest shall be your own to eat and to re-seed your fields." He responded creatively and treated the people with integrity and dignity. He made them self-sufficient. Did they buy into the plan? Did it work? Read for yourself.

"You have saved our lives!" they exclaimed. Because of the man Joseph was, they believed in him, they listened to him, they accepted his plan, they sacrificed and worked hard, and they were grateful.

Leadership calls for the stretching of creativity. If you are a leader, you will occasionally find yourself up against a blank wall. It's big and intimidating and usually tall and slick. You can't push through it, climb over it, or see your way around it. That's when it gets exciting! That's when innovative juices start to flow and you begin to think about possible ways to get beyond that wall. Innovation and creativity (not to mention courage) team up, determined to find an answer and a way. Reminds me of the response of the marine officer in the Korean War. He and his troops found themselves flanked by the enemy on either side as well as out in front of them and not far behind them. Totally surrounded and outnumbered, he responded, "Outstanding . . . they'll never get away this time!"

As a result of his innovative plan, fueled by creativity and courage, Joseph established a policy: "And Joseph made it a statute concerning the land of Egypt valid to this day." That often seems to be the ultimate result: Innovation that leads to a successful plan becomes a workable policy.

In order to think creatively, you have to have room. Remember that, those of you who hold influence in organizations and companies and businesses.

Give everyone around you plenty of room for creativity! Allow opportunities for brainstorming, free from the limitations of suspicion.

Frank Goble's words again come to mind. He offers this wise counsel:

> The best way to kill creativity is to select suspicious, critical, insecure, defensive people as supervisors at every level. At their inception most ideas are delicate and fragile, and require careful nurturing. This is the reason, of course, that men experienced in developing organizational creativity stress creative climate. . . .[7]

Freedom to think! Charles Clark, one of the leading exponents of brainstorming, writes in his book on that subject that there's a bell he rings in the midst of the brainstorming sessions if someone uses a "killer phrase." Novel idea, isn't it? Why not? "Killer phrases" ruin meetings!

Are you ready for some of the killer phrases I've heard during my thirty-five-plus years in Christian leadership?

- It won't work.

- We haven't the time.

- We don't have the personnel to pull it off.

- It's not in the budget.

- We're going to get too much criticism.

- The board isn't going to buy it.

- We've tried that before.

- We've never done that before.

- We're not ready for it yet.

- We'll lose a lot of high donors if we do that.

- All right in theory, but can you put it into practice?

- This could result in a lawsuit.

- It's too modern.

- It's too old-fashioned.

- So and so tried that and failed.

- We're too small for that.

- We're too big for that.

- It costs too much money.

- People won't accept it.

Just as there are "grace killers" and "joy killers" on the loose, so there are "creativity killers," and they are notorious for using "killer phrases." Afraid of risk, they live their frightened lives playing it safe, running scared of being misunderstood. Every major breakthrough comes through hard work—and sometimes even misunderstanding. If you're creative you'll quickly discover there are consequences.

When Marconi told his friends that he had discovered a way to send messages through the air without wires or other physical means, they had him committed to a psychiatric ward. When Samuel Morse asked Congress for $30,000 to implement an experimental telegraph line between Washington D.C., and Baltimore, he was openly ridiculed. (One member of Congress sarcastically moved that the money be spent to construct a railroad to the moon.) Back in 1926, when a young salesman suggested that his company's sales could be increased by using zippers in the front of men's trousers instead of buttons, everyone convulsed with laughter. Eventually, that company became Talon Manufacturing and owed its survival to a single, creative invention—the zipper!

Not all ideas are good ones, of course. I came across an interesting book called the *Incomplete Book of Failures,* which lists the most unsuccessful inventors of all time; it's hilarious. Between 1962 and 1977, Arthur Paul Pedrick patented 162 inventions, none of which are in use today. Among them was a bicycle with amphibious capacity. Another was an arrangement whereby a car could be driven from the backseat. (Some of you may already have cars like that.) In order to irrigate deserts of the world, Pedrick suggested and planned a way to send a constant supply of snowballs from the polar regions through a network of giant pea shooters! He also patented several golf inventions, including a golf ball that could be steered in flight! (I have no idea why that idea never took off.)[8]

I realize creativity can be taken to ridiculous extremes, so don't write me! I'm not suggesting ridiculous decisions, but sometimes you have to consider the ridiculous in order to arrive at an innovative, creative plan. Some folks become so negative, so closed, so restrictive in their thinking, so unbelievably danger-conscious or suspicious, they allow no room for ideas to grow, even from their own children. I remember some of the ingenious plans our kids came up with for handling chores. Dishes, for example. They were convinced that using nothing but paper plates and cups and plastic utensils would really expedite things in the kitchen. Cynthia and I didn't fully embrace that one, but there were times we temporarily accepted their plan!

Christians especially can be threatened by anything "new." I'm not suggesting new theology, understand. As I've said for decades, we need to be willing to leave the familiar methods without disturbing the essential message. Many say they are, but they aren't—not really. Too bad. The right kind of innovation, for example, can wonderfully enhance worship. So many new and fresh approaches can transform our gatherings and make places of worship, once again, attractive and winsome.

Behind changes, I repeat, must be a solid foundation. *The first and highest priority must be our commitment to sound biblical truth and principles.* When we fudge on truth or principles, we don't even start to succeed. Rather, a subtle erosion occurs and we begin to lose. If our plan requires deception, if it means lying, if it calls for mistreatment of others, or if, in any way, it requires us to soften our theology, it's spurious. My advice? Dump it now, not later.

Second, *we must carefully invest our time.* Peter Drucker has said many helpful things, but one of my all-time favorite quotes of his is this:

> Nothing else perhaps distinguishes effective executives as much as their tender loving care of time . . . Unless he manages himself effectively,

no amount of ability, skill, experience, or knowledge will make an executive effective.[9]

We must be able to say no without a lengthy explanation. That means saying no to good things, no to enjoyable things, and no even to marvelous opportunities if our time limitation, based on higher priorities, leaves no room for such. I must answer fifty or more letters a week, inviting me to be involved in various activities or meetings or speaking engagements—most of them edifying and outstanding opportunities. My already established priorities force me to say no to virtually every one of them. That is never easy nor is it enjoyable, but it is right. A principle I learned back in the 1950s still applies: Certain things *must* be so that other things *might* be.

Third, *we must guard our motives*. We must constantly watch how we respond and relate to people, and we must continually ask why we are answering yes or no. Are we doing the "right" thing for the wrong reason? Are we hoping to benefit from our answer? Are we just pleasing people? Sometimes our motive is based on a longstanding habit. Many prefer a rut, but I've discovered that a rut is nothing more than a grave with the ends kicked out. It's a wonderful way to die long before you stop breathing. If you find yourself in the holding pattern of a dull routine lifestyle, perhaps it's time to take a hard look at life through the eyes of Joseph. Stop and think of the adjustments, the changes, the flexibility he demonstrated throughout his years as a leader. Realize that, though he grew older, he refused to run from life's challenges.

As I think of all this, I think of the cross, where all four of these principles were at work. Before that great moment of redemption ever happened, God our Father planned ahead with wise objectivity prompted by His unconditional love. He saw us as we were, not just as He wanted us to be. We were depraved, lost, sinful, spiritually dead. We were aliens. We hated Him. Had we been given a choice in our lost condition, every one of us would have participated in the crucifixion of His Son. He saw us as we were.

Then, His Son, Jesus Christ, submitted with a loyal accountability to the Father's authority. "Yes, I'll go. Yes, I'll carry salvation's message. Yes,

I'll go to this earth that We have made. Yes, I'll be the scourge. I'll be the object of mockery. Yes, I will die. I will submit."

In the cross, the Lord God arranged a plan for our spiritual survival with divine integrity. It required the sacrifice of Christ on the cross. He followed through. We can take Him at His word. He was who He said He was, and He did what He said He would do. With a single heart and a single mind and a single will, He fulfilled the Father's plan.

Finally, Jesus Christ carried out the most innovative, creative plan this world will ever know. From the virgin birth to the death and the resurrection to the soon-coming of Christ, the plan of Almighty God is rich with innovation and creativity. It had never been done before. It will never be done again. It was a once and for all Master Plan only the Creator could envision.

As He did with Joseph, the Father does with us. In His great arrangement of life, He does not discount man's sin; He deals with it. He deals with the hard questions of life. Not questions like how do I make a living, but how do I make a life? Not how do I spend my time, but how do I spend eternity? And not so much how do I get along with the person who sits next to me, but ultimately, how do I get along with God? When we answer the hard questions correctly, all the others fall into place.

May we be models of diligence, honesty, compassion, creativity. May our work be an extension of our integrity. And may each one of us who names the name of Christ as our Lord be a positive influence on those around us and a faithful representative and ambassador for Him who loved us and gave Himself for us.

In other words, may we follow in the footsteps of Joseph. Or, better than that, the footsteps of Jesus.

CHAPTER TWELVE

Highlights of Twilight and Midnight

My day began very early that morning, long before daybreak, with the ringing of the phone. On the other end of the line was the excited, ecstatic voice of a young man who was calling to tell me that a few minutes earlier he had become a father. The baby was fine. The mother was fine but exhausted. The new daddy was fine and ecstatic! He told me the baby's name and the reason they chose the name and all the things related to the birth. He giggled a little and he laughed several times. He shouted a time or two. As I hung up the phone, I smiled. What a joyous way to begin the new day.

After breakfast, I went to the office. About 9:30, I received a call from a couple with an urgent need. They had just gotten news that the wife had been diagnosed with a terminal condition. I was forced to change hats immediately as I ministered to these dear folks. My early-morning smile of delight changed pretty swiftly to a midmorning feeling of sorrow and helplessness. (Several months later, this woman did go to be with the Lord.)

At midday, my lunch was cut short because I had to put the finishing touches on a funeral message that I was to deliver that afternoon at 2:00.

Already, in the space of a few hours, I had gone from birth to critical illness to the grief of a bereaved family at the funeral service.

When I returned to my office, I discovered a note waiting for me, asking me to meet immediately with a couple for counseling. They had been married for a little over ten years and had three children. Now, they said, they were no longer able to communicate; they had separated and were considering divorce. Another change of hats. As we talked, the room was filled with the tears of frustration and angry words. It was an unhappy, unsatisfying encounter. (The husband and wife were unable to resolve their differences and later did divorce.) The whole thing made me sad.

That night, about 7:00, when I reached in the closet to take out my wedding tuxedo, I felt like canceling the evening event. I couldn't, of course, and so I changed hats again. I performed the ceremony, smiled for the photographer, shook the groom's hand, congratulated the proud parents, kissed the bride, and did my best to enter into the gaiety and delight of that evening wedding and happy reception.

Afterward, I slumped into my car—totally spent. As I drove home, I flipped on the radio. Tammy Wynette was singing "I Beg Your Pardon—I Never Promised You a Rose Garden"! I nodded my head in agreement.

Joseph's life was anything but a rose garden, and our journey through it has been anything but boring. His ups and downs were as extreme as my day had been, only a whole lot worse. His was more like a lifelong roller coaster. He was adored, protected, and pampered by his father as he grew up in a hostile environment full of angry brothers. They so envied him that they considered killing him, so they threw him into a pit in Canaan. Deciding rather to make a handful of shekels off him, they sold him to slave traders, who carried him off to Egypt, where he was purchased by a high-ranking official named Potiphar. In this man's household, Joseph was respected and promoted to head steward, given full authority due to the official's trust. Soon he caught the eye of his boss's lecherous wife. Obedient to his God, and determined to maintain his purity, Joseph staunchly resisted her wiles and escaped her advances—only to hear the cries of the woman as she screamed of sexual assault and attempted rape. As a result of her false accusations, he wound up in an Egyptian dungeon, but there, once again, he was trusted and respected. Though he did not harm but, in fact, helped others out, he remained forgotten for several years. Then, through God-ordained circumstances, he was lifted out of that place and virtually overnight elevated to the position of prime minister, Pharaoh's right-hand man. Amazingly, he was back on top. Finally, after a separation of more than twenty years from his family in Canaan, Joseph was reunited with his brothers and his father, even as he was successfully managing the crisis situation brought on by a famine in Egypt.

Despair. Triumph. Heights. Depths. Dreams. Dungeons. Promotion. Rejection. Gain. Loss. The ups and downs, the ins and outs, the powerful reality of this man's life was enough to eclipse anything you and I have ever experienced. Sometimes such contrasts cause men and women to forget God. Sometimes they become so severe and cynical that they decide to abandon old friends and turn against their own family. Not so with Joseph. Life's extremities, rather than erasing his memories of home, only deepened them.

Former pastor and writer, Clarence Edward Macartney, captures this thought with an exquisite touch of creative imagination:

> Great in the dreams of youth, great in the adversities and trials through which he had passed, great in the hour of temptation, Joseph is greatest of all in his prosperity, when his dreams have come true.
>
> He never forgot his father's house. Sometimes when he was handling his great business for Pharaoh, the lords and officers would ask him a question, and Joseph would not answer. He had not heard the question. He was hearing the voice of Jacob, the voice of Benjamin. Sometimes when he was sitting at ease in his palace, a look of abstraction would come over his countenance, and his wife, the daughter of the priest of On, would shake him by the arm, and ask him if he had forgotten her; or she would place Ephraim on one knee and Manasseh on the other knee, and tell them to call home his wandering thoughts and think of her and of his sons. But Joseph's thoughts were far away from that beautiful palace. He saw not the red sandstone columns twined about with serpents, and surmounted by great eagles in whose eyes and in whose talons flashed precious stones. He saw not the far off

winding Nile, nor the huge Pyramids, nor the silent staring Sphinx. Joseph's thoughts were far away from Egypt, at the black tents of Hebron, for "'Mid pleasures and palaces though we may roam, Be it ever so humble there's no place like home.'"[1]

Eventually, the seven-year, treacherous famine ended. Prosperity returned and Egypt blossomed. The fertile Nile delta area, where Joseph had settled his family, began to produce. Year after year, bumper crops were gathered in harvest. For seventeen years Joseph enjoyed both the blessings of God and this bounty from the fields alongside his reunited family.

JACOB: SICKNESS, BLESSING, DEATH

> Now Israel lived in the land of Egypt, in Goshen, and they acquired property in it and were fruitful and became very numerous. And Jacob lived in the land of Egypt seventeen years; so the length of Jacob's life was one hundred and forty-seven years.
>
> Genesis 47:27–28

Jacob's people, now called by his God-given name, Israel, became abundantly fruitful. Young couples married, babies were born, and their numbers greatly increased. Then, after seventeen years in the land of Egypt, Jacob marked his 147th birthday. He, like his favorite son, had known numerous ups and downs, many failures yet many blessings from his forgiving Lord. I agree with Alexander Whyte: "There was no Old Testament saint of them all who, first and last, saw more of the favour and forgiveness of God than Jacob."[2] His journey was nearing the end. Who knows? Maybe the entire clan gathered for a large birthday party. What a celebration it must have been!

Sometime after this, possibly within that same year since that is the last age recorded for him, Jacob realized that the angel of death was near his bedside. Not surprisingly, he called Joseph in. The scene was another of those memorable occasions caught in a scriptural freeze frame.

Jacob with Joseph

When the time for Israel to die drew near, he called his son Joseph and said to him, "Please, if I have found favor in your sight, place now your hand under my thigh and deal with me in kindness and faithfulness. Please do not bury me in Egypt, but when I lie down with my fathers, you shall carry me out of Egypt and bury me in their burial place." And he [Joseph] said, "I will do as you have said." And he [Jacob/ Israel] said, "Swear to me." So he [Joseph] swore to him. Then Israel bowed in worship at the head of the bed.

Genesis 47:29–31

"Swear to me, Joseph—promise me this," Jacob said. "Place your hand under my thigh and swear."

Making promises to the dying is nothing unusual. That is still done today. Frequently I have heard spouses or children tell of promises they made to a dying mate or a parent. But what about this strange gesture of placing one's hand under the thigh of another? What's that all about?

Brown, Driver, and Briggs, old but still reputable authorities on the Hebrew text, suggest that this sealing of the promise was done by placing the hand beneath the lower back or beneath the buttocks. Joseph promised to do as his father asked, and he also indicated this symbolically by placing his hand under Jacob. It was an oath-taking posture common at that time.

"Promise me before our God, Joseph, that you will bury me back in my father's land. Promise to bury me over there in Canaan, the land of our people, not here in Egypt. God brought us to Egypt so we could survive the famine, but I want to be buried in the land of our forefathers, along with Abraham and Isaac and Leah. Take me back there. Don't bury me in Egypt. Swear before God that will not happen." And Joseph swore to keep this promise to his father.

In James Dobson's book *Straight Talk to Men and Their Wives*, Jim tells about the epitaph he placed on his own father's tombstone. On that "footstone," as he calls it, he had two simple but powerful words engraved: "He prayed."[3]

On Jacob's tombstone, Joseph could have placed the words: "He worshiped." Years earlier, of course, "He deceived" might have seemed more appropriate, but now that Jacob was almost a century-and-a-half old, he had come a long way with God. At the end of his life, one of his final acts was to worship the God he had both wrestled with and served. In his old age he urged Joseph to remember that Canaan—not Egypt—was the Promised Land, so he made his son promise to make his final grave there.

Jacob with Joseph's Sons

This scene is followed quickly by another scene of touching significance as Joseph's sons, Manasseh and Ephraim, were brought in to see their dying grandfather.

Manasseh and Ephraim were not little boys; by now, they were young men. Seventeen years had passed since Jacob came to Egypt, and Joseph's sons had been born even before that occurred. Jacob starts by reiterating the covenant God made with him.

> "And now your two sons, who were born to you in the land of Egypt before I came to you in Egypt, are mine; Ephraim and Manasseh shall be mine, as Reuben and Simeon are." . . .
>
> Now the eyes of Israel were so dim from age that he could not see. Then Joseph brought them close to him, and he kissed them and embraced them. And Israel said to Joseph, "I never expected to see your face, and behold, God has let me see your children as well." . . .
>
> But Israel stretched out his right hand and laid it on the head of Ephraim, who was the younger, and his left hand on Manasseh's head, crossing his hands, although Manasseh was the first-born. And he blessed Joseph, and said,
>
> "The God before whom my fathers Abraham and Isaac walked,
> The God who has been my shepherd all my life to this day,
> The angel who has redeemed me from all evil,
> Bless the lads;
> And may my name live on in them,

And the names of my fathers Abraham and Isaac;
And may they grow into a multitude in the midst of the earth."

Genesis 48:5, 10–11, 14–16

Because Joseph had been a special son to Jacob, Joseph's sons were special to their grandfather as well. The NIV study notes on this portion of the text state that Jacob, at his death, adopted Joseph's first two children as his own and in doing that divided Joseph's inheritance in the land of Canaan between them. "Joseph's first two sons would enjoy equal status with Jacob's first two sons [Reuben and Simeon] and in fact would eventually supersede them. Because of an earlier sinful act, Reuben would lose his birthright to Jacob's favorite son, Joseph, and thus to Joseph's sons."[4]

All of this becomes greatly significant later in the history of the nation of Israel, and it makes this last scene with Jacob and his grandsons extremely important.

Perhaps it is my own practical nature, but I see something of great value for us here also. It has to do with how and where Jacob died in contrast to how and where we die. Jacob died on his own bed, at home. Rarely does that occur today. We have fallen upon strange times. Birth has become more and more of a family affair, often with the entire family being present in the "birth suite" when the baby is born. Wonderful change from the way things used to be! On the other hand, death has become relegated more and more to the cold and sometimes uncaring comfort of professionals and the sterile environment of a busy hospital, and, later, the funeral home, or graveside chapel. Only in recent years have we begun to see the hospice movement growing, where people are allowed to spend their last days at home with those they love alongside to support them and encourage them in their final earthly journey.

Yet even with this resurgence of personal, familiar presence, how seldom it is that we see anyone die. Is it any wonder that psychologists tell us that the last place a person can ever envision himself or herself is in a coffin? Where do the dying go? They go to professional places. Only on the rarest occasions do they die with family members (including grandchildren!) encircling them. And while many of those professional places are clean and staffed by competent and even caring people, they can feel like the loneliest spots on earth.

Joe Bayly, who I mentioned earlier regarding the loss of three children and other loved ones, wrote about death with a great deal of understanding, compassion, and authority. Though his words today may be a bit dated, most of us can identify with his comments as he draws this vivid contrast of scenes:

> One of my early memories is of being led into my grandmother's room at Gettysburg, Pennsylvania, to give her a final kiss. . . .
>
> That scene impresses me today with its Old Testament quality. Grandma, an imposing person, was conscious, slightly raised on a bolster, her white hair braided and carefully arranged on the quilt that she had made as a young woman. The bed, a four-poster, was the one in which she had slept for fifty years, in which her four children had been conceived and born.
>
> The wide-boarded floor creaked its familiar creak, the kerosene lamp flickered on the massive bureau, a bouquet of sweet peas from Grandma's garden made the room faintly fragrant.
>
> The old lady was surrounded by her children and grandchildren. In a few hours she died.
>
> Forty years later my children were with their grandfather when he had his last heart attack. We gave him oxygen, called the doctor, and then the ambulance came. The men put Grandpa on a stretcher, carried him out of the house, and that was the last his grandchildren ever saw of him. Children are excluded from most hospitals.
>
> In the intensive care unit of the hospital, my wife and I were with him until the visiting hours were over. The mechanics of survival—tubes, needles, oxygen system, electronic pacemaker—were in him and on him and around him.
>
> Grandpa died alone, at night, after visiting hours. His grandsons had no chance to give him a final kiss, to feel the pressure of his hand on their heads.
>
> In this generation death has moved out of the home to the hospital . . .[5]

As a pastor, and currently one who is training those who will become pastors, I care deeply about this matter of dying. We don't prepare for dying while we're dying. We must prepare for dying while we're living and healthy. We think about it and discuss it together as a family. Death is not something to be feared, shunned, or avoided. It is something to be shared with those family members and friends who have accompanied us through life's sojourn.

Joseph's sons were with their grandfather as he approached those final moments. They felt his hand on their foreheads and heard his tender, wise words of blessing. "May God bless the nation as He blesses you." What a moment! Perhaps Manasseh and Ephraim were kneeling beside their granddad. What a lasting impact for good on the lives of those two young men!

Jacob with His Own Sons

> Then Jacob summoned his sons and said, "Assemble yourselves that I
> may tell you what shall befall you in the days to come.
> Gather together and hear, O sons of Jacob;
> And listen to Israel your father."
>
> Genesis 49:1–2

Despite his age and infirmity, Jacob's memory was nothing short of remarkable. He could name each one of his boys, and he could describe their individual natures and recall with pertinent detail the lives they had lived. Although he had not always disciplined them appropriately or wisely, he knew his sons well. No doubt the Lord assisted at this touching moment of his life by providing the prophetic insight passed on by this aging father. From the firstborn, Reuben, through the youngest, Benjamin, Jacob blessed not only his sons, but the twelve tribes that would descend from them.

> All these are the twelve tribes of Israel, and this is what their father
> said to them when he blessed them. He blessed them, every one with
> the blessing appropriate to him.
>
> Genesis 49:28

After this, Jacob gave them specific instructions about where he was to be buried, in keeping with the promise Joseph had made to him earlier. And then, this beautiful statement: "When Jacob finished charging his sons, he drew his feet into the bed and breathed his last, and was gathered to his people" (Genesis 49:33).

Those who have eternal hope, though grieving over the instant loss death brings, and the painful absence that follows, must remember and be comforted by the realization that when the believer is taken from this life, he or she is gathered into the place of the saints. As it says, Jacob was "gathered to his people." Absent from the body, face to face with the Lord. How simple yet how sacred the moment. With one quiet and final sigh, the old patriarch joined the eternal ranks of departed saints.

John Donne, seventeenth-century English poet, was not only one of that country's great poets but also one of her most celebrated preachers. He wrote eloquently about death:

> All mankinde is of one Author, and is one volume; when one Man dies, one Chapter is not torne out of the booke, but translated into a better language; and every Chapter must be so translated. God emploies several translators: some peeces are translated by age, some by sicknesse, some by warre, some by justice; but God's hand is in every translation; and his hand shall binde up all our scattered leaves againe, for that Librarie where every booke shall lie open to one another.[6]

God translates the life of an individual after death, and *only then* can we measure the significance of that life. Alas, we often realize that significance too late. Most often it is long after that person's death.

JOSEPH: GRIEF, GRACE, GLORY

As Jacob was gathered to his people, Joseph was left to grieve. Whoever has endured the loss of a loving and faithful father, as I have, knows only too well the grip of grief that tightens itself around you. I can still remember feeling strangely orphaned and so alone, though I had the tenderness of my beloved wife, who wept beside me, as well as our four growing children, and my loving brother and sister. Nevertheless, there I was and there he lay, gone from this earth forever. To glory, yes, but from my earthly life. I would never again hear his voice, his laughter, his counsel, his prayers. I would never again share some happy moment with him or feel the touch of his strong hand on my arm or watch him sign his name in his beautiful handwriting. He would never again hold one of my children in his arms or wrap those arms around me in an embrace of affirmation or comfort. Do I understand Joseph's surge of grief? More than I can possibly describe.

I find the following words deeply touching.

> Then Joseph fell on his father's face, and wept over him and kissed him. And Joseph commanded his servants the physicians to embalm his father. So the physicians embalmed Israel. Now forty days were required for it, for such is the period required for embalming. And the Egyptians wept for him seventy days.
>
> Genesis 50:1–3

This reference is not surprising since, if the pyramids and mummies are any example, the Egyptians had developed a sophisticated system of embalming. After the physicians had completed the unique process, which took forty days, and after the people had mourned his passing for seventy days, the funeral procession began its long journey to Canaan.

Interestingly, the Egyptians, as well as Joseph and all his Hebrew family, mourned. Out of love and respect for the man who had endeared himself to them and earned such a sterling reputation among them, the Egyptians, from Pharaoh on down, felt his loss. They, too, wept those seventy days. Furthermore, when it came time for Joseph to keep his promise and bury his father in faraway Canaan, the Egyptian monarch looked with favor upon the entire procedure.

Burial of His Father

> And when the days of mourning for him were past, Joseph spoke to the household of Pharaoh, saying, "If now I have found favor in

your sight, please speak to Pharaoh, saying, 'My father made me swear, saying, "Behold, I am about to die; in my grave which I dug for myself in the land of Canaan, there you shall bury me." Now therefore, please let me go up and bury my father; then I will return.'" And Pharaoh said, "Go up and bury your father, as he made you swear." So Joseph went up to bury his father, and with him went up all the servants of Pharaoh, the elders of his household and all the elders of the land of Egypt, and all the household of Joseph and his brothers and his father's household; they left only their little ones and their flocks and their herds in the land of Goshen. There also went up with him both chariots and horsemen; and it was a very great company.

Genesis 50:4–9

This great company of people must have made an impressive funeral procession, silently wending its way out from Egypt, then eastward across the parched wilderness of Sinai, and finally turning north toward the God-given region called the Promised Land, I wonder what folks thought as they saw the procession pass those several days? There goes a great king? There goes the father of Joseph? There goes the body of him through whose loins the nation of the Jews has been sustained? Some desert-dwelling Bedouins may have merely stood to their feet, out of respect, and stared. What an epochal moment, another ending to another era. It is fitting at this point in the story that the narrative slows to the mournful cadence of Jacob's funeral procession.

Once they arrived at their destination, they buried Jacob as he had desired, in the cave of Machpelah, the burial site of his forebears, Abraham and Sarah, Isaac and Rebekah, as well as his wife, Leah.

Despite the prominence of Joseph in the government of Egypt, the family would never consider its inheritance to be in Egypt. The legitimacy of their claim to Canaan lay with the divine gift of the land to Abraham, the first forefather of Israel. . . . The return of the funeral cortege from Egypt for Jacob's burial there renewed the family's claim

to the cave, and also to the land. It was a pledge that they would one
day return to occupy what had in fact been bestowed on Abraham
and Sarah, Isaac and Rebekah. Leah too was buried there (but not
Rachel), and Jacob would take his place in the family mausoleum, as
one of the three great names for ever associated with God's promise
of the land: Abraham, Isaac and Jacob.[7]

The significant site prompted even more tears from the son who missed
his father terribly. I'm so grateful we're not shielded by the Scriptures from
this very tender and vulnerable side of Joseph's nature. How very sad he
was to lose his beloved father!

> When they came to the threshing floor of Atad, which is beyond
> the Jordan, they lamented there with a very great and sorrowful
> lamentation; and he observed seven days mourning for his father.
> . . . And after he had buried his father, Joseph returned to Egypt,
> he and his brothers, and all who had gone up with him to bury
> his father.
>
> Genesis 50:10, 14

The return to Egypt must have included long moments of reflection.
Perhaps Joseph and his brothers sat around a fire late into the night, where
the caravan had stopped for rest, and recalled various scenes from the past.
Recovering from grief takes time—months, sometimes years. And in this
case, some of those reflective occasions stirred renewed twinges of guilt
in the brothers' hearts. And once that old taskmaster of the conscience
resurfaced, fear and anxiety weighed them down.

> When Joseph's brothers saw that their father was dead, they said,
> "What if Joseph should bear a grudge against us and pay us back in
> full for all the wrong which we did to him!" So they sent a message
> to Joseph, saying, "Your father charged before he died, saying, 'Thus
> you shall say to Joseph, "Please forgive, I beg you, the transgression of
> your brothers and their sin, for they did you wrong." 'And now, please

forgive the transgression of the servants of the God of your father."
And Joseph wept when they spoke to him.

Genesis 50:15–17

Forgiveness of His Brothers

This is another glimpse into the gentle and tender side of Joseph. Their wrestlings over past (and already forgiven!) sins moved him to tears. They still couldn't appropriate grace. It was still "too good to be true." Everything they had said and done so many years ago came rushing back into their minds. Fear also returned as their imagination took charge. Had Joseph been kind to them only for their father's sake? Was that the reason he had not yet taken his revenge upon them?

There was no doubt in their minds that the death of their father could mean the sudden removal of a restraining influence on their brother. As long as Jacob was there, they felt safe, or at least safer. With him gone, who knew what might happen? Once again guilt did a number on them. Perhaps in their own mourning of their father's passing, as their hearts were especially softened, guilt slipped in the unguarded gate of their memory and again robbed them of their fragile peace.

They were rehearsing past sin that had already been fully forgiven by Joseph, but which had not been fully forgotten by them. As a result, they were afraid of Joseph. So they sent him a message, telling him that their father had asked that Joseph forgive them for what they had done.

Joseph's response once again reveals his character. He wept when they said this to him, because they hadn't completely believed what he had said earlier. Remember when he told them that there was a divine purpose behind everything that had happened to him? Remember when he told them that it was not they who had sent him to Egypt, but God? He realized as they stumbled through their words and attempted to rehash all the garbage of the past that they really hadn't heard him or believed him. He needed to repeat those words yet again.

Without hesitation he offered them reassurance in the form of forgiveness. Joseph's words here in Genesis 50 provide the finest expression of forgiveness we find anywhere, outside of the words of Jesus Christ himself. I suggest you read them slowly and with feeling, preferably aloud. All who wrestle with needless guilt over forgiven sins will benefit from frequent reminders of Joseph's response. I would suggest memorizing these few lines so that they become etched forever on your mind. Hopefully, they will help you to comprehend and appropriate the grace of God as never before in your life. Joseph reassured his brothers:

> "Do not be afraid, for am I in God's place? And as for you, you meant evil against me, but God meant it for good in order to bring about this present result, to preserve many people alive. So therefore, do not be afraid; I will provide for you and your little ones." So he comforted them and spoke kindly to them.
>
> Genesis 50:19–21

"Am I in God's place?" Joseph asked them. Had he been a lesser man, he could have played "king of the mountain" and filled the role of God. "Grace killers" do that sort of thing, you know. They exploit the power they have over others. They play a carnal game when they have someone cornered, someone who is vulnerable and at their mercy.

Joseph refused to do that. He didn't do it earlier at their reunion, and he doesn't do it now. In his obedience to God, he was restrained by feelings of tender mercy as he communicated God's grace. "Am I in God's place?" he asked his brothers, saying, in effect, "Brothers, listen to me. Let's get this cleared up for the last time. I know what you did, and I know what you meant by it. I know you meant to do me evil. Okay? I understand all that. That was your plan. But God had other plans, and He turned the results of your evil intentions into something good. At one time I did not understand all this, but that time is long past. Get this straight—God meant it all for good." Joseph never stood taller than at this moment in his life. As Churchill would say, it was his "finest hour."

A helicopter pilot once told me of a magnificent experience he'd had when he was flying a police helicopter. For the first and only time in his life, he said, he saw a complete rainbow. All we usually ever see in a rainbow is an arc, with one end (or both) fixed to the earth. But that is only half the rainbow, the pilot told me, because a rainbow is circular. He said, "When I was in just the right position at just the right spot in that heavenly prism, I not only saw it, but *I flew through it and around it*. It was a once-in-a-lifetime moment," he said, "as I was entering into this rainbow."

"So there's no pot of gold at the end of it?" I joked.

"No," he said. "Because there is no end to it."

Joseph said to his brothers, "I see the whole rainbow. You guys are only able to see part of it. But I tell you, I have been through it and around it and there is no end. You meant it for evil, but God meant it for good." The gold was in Joseph, quite frankly, not sitting in some imaginary pot.

Guard your heart when you have the power to place guilt on someone else. Refuse to rub their nose in the mess they've made. Remember the father of the Prodigal Son. Best of all, remember Joseph. "Don't be afraid," he comforted them kindly. "I will provide for you and your children."

I love the words of George Robinson's timeless hymn:

> Loved with everlasting love,
> Led by grace that love to know;
> Gracious Spirit from above,
> Thou hast taught me it is so!
> O, this full and perfect peace!
> O, this transport all divine!
> In a love which cannot cease,
> I am His, and He is mine.[8]

My favorite line in that hymn is, "Led by grace that love to know." It is especially pertinent here, because it so beautifully describes Joseph, who, like Christ, had a love that would not cease.

Joseph was led by grace. He spoke by grace. He forgave by grace. He forgot by grace. He loved by grace. He remembered by grace. Because of grace, when his brothers bowed before him in fear, he could say, "Get on your feet! God meant it all for good."

Completion of His Life

What a way to bring someone's life to a close! The Spirit of God wastes no time moving from Joseph's significant expression of grace to his last words.

God's timepiece finally ticks to the end of his magnificent life, as we transition from Joseph's finest hour to Joseph's final words. Right up to the end, the man is a joy to be around. No complaining, no whining, no regrets. And to the very end, he was thinking of others. Rather than calling attention to all that he had achieved—which was enormous—he reminded them of what God had promised—which was eternal.

> And Joseph said to his brothers, "I am about to die, but God will surely take care of you, and bring you up from this land to the land which He promised on oath to Abraham, to Isaac and to Jacob." Then Joseph made the sons of Israel swear, saying, "God will surely take care of you, and you shall carry my bones up from here." So Joseph died at the age of one hundred and ten years; and he was embalmed and placed in a coffin in Egypt.
>
> Genesis 50:24–26

When Joseph knew he was about to die and was, in fact, ready to die, he once more reassured his family. He had not forgotten God's promises, and, like his father, Jacob, he did not want his family to forget either.

"God will continue to care for you," he said, "and someday He will take you back to the land of our forefathers, the land of Canaan." He then asked them to swear not only that they believed this, but that when it happened, they would carry his bones back with them.

Then, at the rich old age of 110 years, almost as quickly as Joseph came on the biblical scene, he passes from it, leaving rich memories of a life of pristine integrity and grace-filled forgiveness.

YOU AND ME: OUR REMAINING YEARS

End of story, end of Genesis, but not end of nation.

Through the life of Joseph we have come to realize that, though centuries removed from us, this was a man who lived out many of our own experiences; and what he learned through his life is as relevant to us today as the evening news—more so in fact! His legacy to us is that he, being dead, still speaks. We've discovered many truths as we've examined the life and character of Joseph. Truths about integrity, about forgiveness, about guilt, about faith, and certainly about grace. But three enduring lessons seem to waft over his life like a fragrant aroma.

First, *God sovereignly works all things for His glory and for our good.* Yes, all things. None of life is insignificant or wasted when lived under the purposeful hand of our loving heavenly Father. I'm convinced that Joseph came to terms with this early in his life, which explains how he could have taken the blows and buffetings that came his way in such abundance. Realizing we operate our lives under the Father's providential care works wonders when the bottom drops out again and again.

Second, *Joseph lived his life free of bitterness despite everything that happened to him,* despite every hard knock that came his way. Even in old age, he was free of bitterness. The tree of his life bore no bitter fruit.

Few things are more difficult or troubling to see than a bitter old person—wrapped in a blanket of anger, spewing forth profanity, poring over albums of wrongs done, and feeding on the dregs of would-be memories.

One woman wrote these penetrating words: "Do they really matter, all the why's? Could all the answers take away the pain, or all the reasons really dry my eyes, though from Heaven's court? No, I would weep again. My God, You have saved me from Hell's black abyss; oh, save me now from the tyranny of bitterness!"

Have the jaws of the "tyranny of bitterness" clamped down on you? Is that the way you want to finish your years? Will that be the memory that is left of your life when you are gone? Don't let it happen! Let's spend our remaining years as Joseph did, reassuring those around us, spreading the contagious charm of grace, claiming the hope-filled promises of God.

My dear friend Ken Gire asks three searching questions, then offers several splendid answers in his book *A Father's Gift: The Legacy of Memories.*

What pictures will my son remember
    when he comes to the plain granite marker
    over his father's grave?
    What will my daughters remember?
    Or my wife?

I've resolved to give fewer lectures,
    to send fewer platitudes rolling their way,
    to give less criticism,
    to offer fewer opinions. . . .

From now on, I'll give them pictures they can live by,
    pictures that can comfort them,
    encourage them,
    and keep them warm
    in my absence.

Because when I'm gone, there will only be
    silence.
    And memories. . . .

Of all
    I could give
    to make their lives a little fuller,
    a little richer,
    a little more prepared for the journey ahead of them,
    nothing compares to the gift of
    remembrance—
    pictures that show they are special
    and that they are loved.

Pictures that will be there
    when I am not.

Pictures that have within them
    a redemption all their own.[9]

Third, *as Joseph faced death, he was right with both man and God.* He had long ago made peace with his brothers, and since it was a peace founded on the mercy of God, it still held. All that was true because he was right with God, not as some distant figure, but as his Lord and Master. Like his forefathers, Joseph had the assurance that, at death, he would be gathered to God's people.

We, too, need to meet death with that assurance, saved from "hell's black abyss." Let those words stick. Without Christ, when death comes, there is nothing but hell and all its horror. In Jesus Christ there is nothing but eternity with God and all its joy. The eternal contrast is as black and white as that. Don't believe any other gray message. When we accept the Savior's death as death on our behalf, then our final twilight and midnight will be turned to a joyous morning that will never end.

CONCLUSION

Joseph: A Man of Integrity and Forgiveness

When I began this biographical series of books on "Great Lives from God's Word," I wondered if I might start to lose the excitement, the delight as time wore on. Not surprisingly, my first volume on *David* held my attention from start to finish. His colorful and dynamic presence stayed strong all the way to the end. I wondered, again, if the enthusiasm might erode as I stepped off that "high" and took on the challenge of a second volume, *Esther*.

No disappointment there! Her courage, her vitality, her willingness to become the link of hope in the long, illustrious legacy of her people enraptured me. I couldn't escape the excitement of seeing God at work, accomplishing His good purposes through each event. One dramatic scene after another surrounded Esther's life. But then, as those pages drew to a close, I was haunted again with those lingering questions: Is that it? Will I ever reach the same level of ecstasy? As two books turn to three, can I expect to experience anywhere near the fulfillment that was mine as I wrote about King David and Queen Esther?

Little did I realize! Having completed, this third volume, *Joseph: A Man of Integrity and Forgiveness,* I have decided to lay my concern aside forever.

Candidly, I do not remember a more enjoyable or fulfilling experience in all my literary career than was mine in the writing of this third biographical work. I mean that with all my heart and without exaggeration. Never have I been more buoyed up in my spirit or strengthened in my soul as I have in the study of this marvelous man named Joseph as God accomplished His will so effectively through him. And the ease with which these chapters have fallen together is nothing short of amazing.

There were moments when I was so lost in the process that I had trouble orienting myself to my surroundings. I'll be even more candid with you: A few times it felt as if Joseph were sitting here at my elbow, with his hand on my shoulder, urging me on, prompting me to write those lines this way, stopping me from saying something that way. Once I laughed out loud at a certain expression I used. It was as if the man leaned over and whispered it in my ear. While I certainly don't believe in automatic writing, I felt guided by the Holy Spirit more than ever before in my life. At times I felt so caught up in the story, I could almost hear the rumbling roll of chariot wheels and see the sphinx outside my window. It was magnificent, and I give God great praise. I don't know what happened, but I hope it starts a trend!

I've neither been tired nor have I once faced a mental block (an author's dread) since I first sat down with my tablet weeks ago. Some days began a little after three in the morning. Others ended near midnight, but sleep had fled from me. I normally need only a little, but during this particular project, I needed even less. *It's been wonderful!* Ideas have flowed freely and the chapters have connected well. Would that all books could be such a pleasure to pen.

Best of all, this has truly been a spiritual experience. There were certain places where I had to pause and allow the application I had just written to others seep into my own needy heart. I found the chapter on keeping a positive attitude especially convicting. Also, reliving the memories of family reunions from years gone by became an emotional journey for me. I needed to revisit those scenes from my own past as I wrote chapter ten. I had almost forgotten how much fun we had as a family. And I will freely admit, I wept my way through much of that final chapter. Sometimes, I had to lay my head down and sob. I don't believe I realized before I wrote of Joseph's grieving the loss of his father, Jacob, how much I needed to finish grieving the loss of my own dad. I thought all that was over. It wasn't. Because of these things, and so much more, Joseph has endeared himself to me as few lives I've ever examined.

Hopefully, by now, you feel a similar kinship with the old prime minister of Egypt, whose remarkable life is enough to make any of us sit up and take notice. Because the experience of writing about him has been so enriching, I find myself unusually motivated to take on another biblical character as we continue our series on "Great Lives" together. But that's another story to be enjoyed at another time. Thanks to Joseph, I can hardly wait to return to my desk with tablet in hand.

For now, let's be grateful for a man God raised up to trust Him in every situation and to model His grace before those who didn't deserve it. My hope is that by reading of Joseph's exemplary spirit and extraordinary skills we will begin to think like he thought and live like he lived. After all, that's the purpose of reading about godly men and women—to break free of those things that have held us hostage and hindered our relationship with Christ and others long enough. Both David and Esther have played vital roles in that process. Along with them comes *Joseph: A Man of Integrity and Forgiveness,* who challenges us to make a difference in our world by being different in our lives—by God's grace and for God's glory.

Join me, won't you?

ENDNOTES

Joseph: A Man of Integrity and Forgiveness

INTRODUCTION

1. David Aikman, *Great Souls: Six Who Changed the Century* (Nashville: Word Publishing, 1998), xii.
2. Ibid., xvi.

CHAPTER ONE

1. Clarence Edward Macartney, *Preaching without Notes* (New York: Abingdon-Cokesbury Press, 1946), 121–122.
2. Naomi H. Rosenblatt and Joshua Horwitz, *Wrestling with Angels* (New York: Delacorte Press, 1995), 315.
3. H. C. Leupold, *Exposition of Genesis*, vol. 2 (Grand Rapids, Mich.: Baker Book House, 1959), 955.
4. *Congressional Quarterly*, quoted in William Bennett, *Index of Leading Cultural Indicators* (New York: Simon & Schuster, 1994), 83.
5. Stephen R. Covey, *The Seven Habits of Highly Effective Families* (New York: Golden Books, 1997), 16–17.

6. Robert G. DeMoss, Jr., *Leaven to Discern* (Grand Rapids, Mich.: Zondervan Publishing House, 1992), 53.

7. F. B. Meyer, *Joseph: Beloved—Hated—Exalted* (Fort Washington, Penn.: Christian Literature Crusade, n.d.), 24.

CHAPTER TWO

1. Dietrich Bonhoeffer, *Temptation* (New York: Macmillan Publishing Co., Collier Books, 1953), 116–117.

2. Meyer, 30.

3. Thomas Carlyle, quoted in *John Bartlett's Familiar Quotations,* ed. Emily Morison Beck (Boston: Little, Brown and Co., 1980), 474.

4. Clarence Edward Macartney, *Trials of Great Men of the Bible* (Nashville: Abingdon Press, 1946), 46–47.

5. Bonhoeffer, 116–117.

6. William Congreve, quoted in *John Bartlett's Familiar Quotations,* 324.

7. Dag Hammarskjold, *Markings,* trans. Lief Sjoberg and W. H. Auden (New York: Alfred A. Knoph, 1965), 15.

CHAPTER THREE

1. Aleksandr Solzhenitsyn, *The Gulag Archipelago: 1918–1956. An Experiment in Literary Investigation,* vol. 3, part 5, chap. 5 (New York: HarperCollins, 1992), 615.

2. Charles Edison, "The Electric Thomas Edison," *Great Lives, Great Deeds* (Pleasantville, N.Y.: Reader's Digest Association, 1964), 200–203.

3. Ibid., 204–205.

4. C. S. Lewis, *The Problem of Pain* (New York: Macmillan Publishing Co., Collier Books, 1962), 93.

5. Philip Yancey, *Where Is God When It Hurts?* (Grand Rapids, Mich.: Zondervan Corp., 1977), 95.

CHAPTER FOUR

1. A. W. Tozer, *The Root of the Righteous* (Camp Hill, Penn.: Christian Publications, Inc., 1986), 137.
2. G. Frederick Owen, *Abraham to the Middle-East Crisis,* 4th ed., rev. (Grand Rapids, Mich.: Wm. B. Eerdmans Publishing Co., 1957), 29.
3. Joseph Bayly, *The Last Thing We Talk About* formerly published as *The View from a Hearse* (Elgin, Ill.: David C. Cook Publishing, Co., 1973), 120–121.

CHAPTER FIVE

1. Saint Francis of Assisi, quoted in *John Bartlett's Familiar Quotations,* 138.
2. J. Oswald Sanders, *Robust in Faith* (Chicago: Moody Press, 1965), 44.
3. Victor P. Hamilton, *The Book of Genesis: Chapters 18–50,* ed. R. K. Harrison (Grand Rapids, Mich.: Wm. B. Eerdmans Publishing Co., 1995), 508.
4. Eugene H. Peterson, *The Message: The New Testament in Contemporary English* (Colorado Springs: NavPress, 1993), 314.
5. Gene Getz, *Joseph: Overcoming Obstacles through Faithfulness* (Nashville: Broadman & Holman, Publishers, 1996), 108.
6. Alexander Whyte, *Bible Characters,* vol. 1 (Grand Rapids, Mich.: Zondervan Publishing House, 1952), 122–123.

CHAPTER SIX

1. Meyer, 69. The "Lethe-stream" Meyer refers to is a "river in Hades whose waters cause drinkers to forget their past" (*Merriam-Webster's Collegiate Dictionary,* Tenth Edition, see "lethe").
2. Leupold, 1053.

3. Eugene H. Peterson, *The Message: The Wisdom Books* (Colorado Springs: NavPress, 1993), 126.
4. William Sangster, quoted in Haddon W. Robinson, *Biblical Preaching* (Grand Rapids, Mich.: Baker Book House, 1980), 150.
5. C. S. Lewis, *Mere Christianity*, rev. ed. (New York: Macmillan Publishing Co., Collier Books, 1952), 72–73.

CHAPTER SEVEN

1. Hamilton, 546.

CHAPTER EIGHT

1. William Shakespeare, *King Henry VI* 5.6.2.
2. Paul Tournier, *Guilt and Grace* (San Francisco: Harper & Row, Publishers, 1962), 93.
3. Henry M. Morris, *The Genesis Record* (Grand Rapids, Mich.: Baker Book House, 1976), 610.
4. Frederick Buechner, *Wishful Thinking: A Theological ABC* (New York: Harper and Row, Publishers, 1973), 33–34.

CHAPTER NINE

1. Deborah Jean Swindoll. Used by permission.
2. John H. Sailhamer, *The Expositor's Bible Commentary*, vol. 2, ed. Frank E. Gaebelein (Grand Rapids, Mich.: Zondervan Publishing House, Regency Reference Library, 1990), 257.
3. John Newton, "Happy in Him," *Christ in Song* (Washington, D.C., 1908).

CHAPTER TEN

1. Hamilton, 587.

2. Douglas MacArthur, quoted in *Quote Unquote,* comp. Lloyd Cory (Wheaton, Ill.: SP Publications, Victor Books, 1977), 15.
3. Alfred Edersheim, *Bible History, Old Testament,* vol. 1 (Grand Rapids, Mich.: Wm. B. Eerdmans Publishing Co., 1959), 175.
4. David Redding, *Jesus Makes Me Laugh* (Grand Rapids, Mich.: Zondervan Publishing House, 1977), 100–102. (Also in *A Rose Will Grow Anywhere* available through Starborne House, PO Box 767, Delaware, OH 43015)
5. James M. Black, "When the Roll Is Called Up Yonder," *The Hymnal for Worship and Celebration* (Waco, Tex.: Word Music, a division of Word, Inc., 1986), 543.

CHAPTER ELEVEN

1. Frank Goble, *Excellence in Leadership* (Thornwood, N.Y.: Caroline House Publishers, 1972), 131.
2. Arthur Maslow, *Motivation and Personality* (New York: Harper & Row, 1954), 257, 207, 203.
3. Arthur Gordon, "A Foolproof Formula for Success," *Reader's Digest* (December, 1966), 88.
4. Warren W. Wiersbe, *The Integrity Crisis* (Nashville: Oliver Nelson, a division of Thomas Nelson Publishers, 1988), 21.
5. Ibid., 21–22.
6. Jerry White, *Honesty, Morality and Conscience* (Colorado Springs: NavPress, 1979), 49.
7. Goble, 29.
8. Stephen Pile, *The Incomplete Book of Failures* (New York: E. P. Dutton, 1979), 22.
9. Peter Drucker, *The Effective Executive* (New York: Harper & Row, 1966), viii.

CHAPTER TWELVE

1. Clarence Edward Macartney, *The Greatest Men of the Bible* (New York: Abingdon Press, [1941]), 108–109.
2. Whyte, *Bible Characters,* vol. 1, 111.

3. James Dobson, *Straight Talk to Men and Their Wives* (Waco, Tex.: Word Books, 1980), 213.
4. Notes, *The NIV Study Bible* (Grand Rapids, Mich.: Zondervan Publishing House, 1985), 78.
5. Bayly, 29–30.
6. John Donne, 17th century poet.
7. Joyce Baldwin, *The Message of Genesis 12–50* (Downers Grove, Ill.: InterVarsity Press, 1986), 214.
8. George W. Robinson, "I Am His and He Is Mine," *The Hymnal for Worship and Celebration* (Waco, Tex.: Word Music, a division of Word, Inc., 1986), 490.
9. Ken Gire, *A Father's Gift: The Legacy of Memories,* formerly published as *The Gift of Remembrance* (Grand Rapids, Mich.: Zondervan Publishing House, 1992), 51, 53, 57.

ABOUT THE AUTHOR

D r. Charles R. Swindoll is senior pastor of Stonebriar Community Church, chancellor of Dallas Theological Seminary, and the Bible teacher on the internationally syndicated radio program *Insight for Living*. He has written more than thirty best-selling books, such as *Strengthening Your Grip*, *Laugh Again*, *The Grace Awakening*, and the million-selling Great Lives from God's Word series. Chuck and his wife, Cynthia, live in Frisco, Texas.

The Great Lives Series

In his Great Lives from God's Word series, Charles R. Swindoll shows us how the great heroes of the faith offer a model of courage, hope, and triumph in the face of adversity.

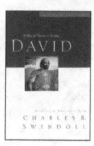

DAVID
A Man of
Passion and
Destiny

ESTHER
A Woman of
Strength and
Dignity

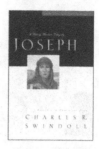

JOSEPH
A Man of
Integrity and
Forgiveness

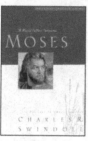

MOSES
A Man of
Selfless
Dedication

ELIJAH
A Man of
Heroism and
Humility

PAUL
A Man of
Grace and Grit

JOB
A Man of
Heroic
Endurance

THOMAS NELSON
Since 1798

thomasnelson.com